What a treasure of truth you have in your hands. Learn it for yourself, and God will use you to help others, even as Nancy does. The Word of God has the answers, and that is exactly where Nancy Guthrie, a woman acquainted with sorrow, takes us. If you let Nancy take you by the hand, lead you where she has been, share with you truth that never changes, and cry, "Heal me, O Lord" (Jeremiah 17:14), you will find yourself "hearing Jesus speak into your sorrow" . . . and there you will find healing.

KAY ARTHUR, co-CEO of Precept Ministries International

My friend Nancy Guthrie has experienced two of the most profound losses that a human heart should ever have to bear, but out of her valley, she's heard his words. Really heard. And she wants to share what she's heard with you. This is no theoretical treatise but a compelling book hammered out on the anvil of a mom's heart. You *will* benefit from hearing these words too!

DENNIS RAINEY, president of FamilyLife and host of *FamilyLife Today*

A mutual friend introduced me to Nancy Guthrie as I was going through a personal crisis of my own. My friend felt certain I would draw strength and hope from hearing how Nancy and her husband, David, were coping with devastating loss. He was so right. She spoke to me where I was living, inspiring me to keep pressing on in spite of my pain. Nancy's style is straightforward, raw, and yet full of faith. This book is for all those who find themselves unable to sleep in the middle of the night due to an ache in their souls. She takes us even further into the existential question most of us ask when we're hurting: Does Jesus *really* know what it's like to have a broken heart? This is a book I'll refer to and recommend often to those struggling with unanswered questions about suffering.

KAY WARREN, executive director of HIV/AIDS Initiative, Saddleback Church

From a crucible of personal tragedy, Nancy Guthrie confronts deep, disturbing questions with unflinching candor. Never content with the usual answers, she digs and digs, for her own soul and ours. Her authentic message of hope challenges and nourishes both mind and heart.

HAROLD MYRA, former executive chairman of Christianity Today International and author of *One Extraordinary Day*

Nancy Guthrie invites us to join her on her journey of grief and loss as she seeks a deeper understanding of Jesus through her pain. Those who read her story will be moved by the tenacity of a grieving mother's faith as she clings to Jesus despite unanswered questions and a sorrow that won't go away.

CAROLYN CUSTIS JAMES, author of *The Gospel of Ruth*

Postmodernity seeks to deny death by driving it into the closet, to trivialize it by treating it irreverently, or to circumvent it through the use of clever clichés. In sharp contrast, Nancy Guthrie writes with the realism and perspective of one who has been refined in the cauldron of life's tragedies. She does not offer up a panacea but the peace that comes from hearing Jesus speak into our sorrows.

HANK HANEGRAAFF, president of the Christian Research Institute and host of the *Bible Answer Man* broadcast

A life crisis is gritty and messy. While books that soothe have their place, you need a real-world guide to finding help and hope when it seems like there is none to be found. This is that book. It will show you, in your darkest of days, how to find healing and rebuild your life.

STEVE GRISSOM, founder of DivorceCare/GriefShare

Nancy writes with both conviction and compassion. . . . She takes on the hard questions that arise from ongoing suffering and undesired outcomes; then she responds to them with Scripture—which she applies to the issues with laser-like clarity. Not only does Nancy lead us to the Word, she also helps us connect with the living Word—Jesus. I highly recommend this thoroughly biblical book to all those who are suffering or helping others in their struggles. I found it a source of strength and encouragement.

SARAH YOUNG, author of *Jesus Calling*

She asks the really hard questions and doesn't skirt around any of them. She reminded me that Jesus does indeed meet us in the worst of circumstances with real answers—not trite, polite sayings that would fit on a motivational calendar but real, HARD, deep truths that have the power to cut through the most awful scenario you could imagine and meet you right there with authentic, genuine hope.

WENDY ALSUP, Practical Theology for Women blog at theologyforwomen.org

Thanks to Nancy Guthrie for writing what needs to be stated and doing so from one who has been there, even more, from one who has grown through the sorrow to maturity . . . . At times, I was back reliving my own experiences . . . nodding my head, even dealing with tears at times, but also having heard Jesus speak into my own sorrow. What a tribute to the author that she could effectively communicate in such a way to bring alongside those who have also suffered.

RICH SHIELDS, President, American Lutheran Theological Seminary

Guthrie encourages even the most wounded person to open their hearts and minds to the practical comforts Christ affords when we follow closely at His side. Christians will drink deeply of the truth that Jesus also has known overwhelming sorrow; has heard God tell Him no; is willing to heal man's deadliest disease; will keep His people safe; will give His followers purpose in their pain; will offer them a heart for forgiveness; will be absolutely enough for each person; He alone gives the life that cannot be taken away; and He is fully in control of both life and death. These amazingly uplifting and encouraging words directly from God's Word will have Christians re-evaluating what they say they believe.

FAITHFULREADER.COM

Hearing
Jesus Speak into
Your Sorrow

❧

NANCY GUTHRIE

author of *Holding On to Hope*

TYNDALE
MOMENTUM®

The nonfiction imprint of
Tyndale House Publishers, Inc.

Visit Tyndale online at www.tyndale.com.

Visit Tyndale Momentum online at www.tyndalemomentum.com.

Visit Nancy Guthrie's website at www.nancyguthrie.com.

TYNDALE, Tyndale Momentum, and Tyndale's quill logo are registered trademarks of Tyndale House Publishers, Inc. The Tyndale Momentum logo is a trademark of Tyndale House Publishers, Inc. Tyndale Momentum is the nonfiction imprint of Tyndale House Publishers, Inc., Carol Stream, Illinois.

Hearing Jesus Speak into Your Sorrow

Designed by Jennifer Ghionzoli

Edited by Stephanie Rische

Unless otherwise indicated, all Scripture quotations are taken from the *Holy Bible,* New Living Translation, second edition, copyright © 1996, 2004, 2007 by Tyndale House Foundation. (Some quotations may be from the NLT, first edition, copyright © 1996.) Used by permission of Tyndale House Publishers, Inc., Carol Stream, Illinois 60188. All rights reserved.

Scripture quotations marked NIV are taken from the Holy Bible, *New International Version,® NIV.®* Copyright © 1973, 1978, 1984 by Biblica, Inc.® Used by permission. All rights reserved worldwide.

Scripture quotations marked *The Message* are taken from *THE MESSAGE,* copyright © 1993, 1994, 1995, 1996, 2000, 2001, 2002 by Eugene H. Peterson. Used by permission of NavPress. All rights reserved. Represented by Tyndale House Publishers, Inc.

Scripture quotations marked NKJV are taken from the New King James Version,® copyright © 1982 by Thomas Nelson, Inc. Used by permission. All rights reserved.

For information about special discounts for bulk purchases, please contact Tyndale House Publishers at csresponse@tyndale.com, or call 1-800-323-9400.

Library of Congress Cataloging-in-Publication Data

Guthrie, Nancy.
   Hearing Jesus speak into your sorrow / Nancy Guthrie.
     p. cm.
   ISBN 978-1-4143-2548-4 (hc)
   1. Suffering—Biblical teaching. 2. Jesus Christ—Words. I. Title.
   BS2545.S9G88 2009
   248.8'6—dc22   2009002212

Printed in China

25   24   23   22   21   20   19
12   11   10   9   8   7   6

DEDICATION

None of us has to look very far to find
people we love who are hurting deeply,
and I am no exception.
I lovingly dedicate this book
to my friends and family
who live with the sorrow of
infidelity, infertility,
a spouse's rejection, a child's rebellion,
paralysis, bipolar disorder, suicide,
depression, dementia, a learning disability, death,
fear over finances, loss of reputation, a difficult marriage,
an unwanted singleness, an embarrassing failure,
an ongoing conflict, a pervasive loneliness.

Know that I am sharing your sorrow,
and I'm listening with you
to hear Jesus speak.

CONTENTS

*So pay attention to how you hear. To those who
listen to my teaching, more understanding will be given.*

—JESUS (LUKE 8:18)

Introduction

There is a significant birthday coming up at my house, and I'm finding myself thinking about it quite often. When I do, I feel a lump forming in my throat, and tears begin to burn behind my eyes.

Soon the day is coming when our daughter, Hope, would be ten. Ten somehow seems significant—more significant than nine or eight and some of the other numbers that have gone by barely acknowledged.

Our daughter's life was marked by days rather than years; she lived 199 days. In other words, there were not nearly enough of them, in my accounting. And as I'm anticipating what would have been her tenth birthday, I'm also anticipating the day that comes 199 days later—the day that will mark a decade since I have held her and known her. It feels like an ever-widening chasm as the years take me further away from her, even as they bring me closer to her.

Honestly I had not known much sorrow in my life before Hope introduced me to it. And one might think that in loving and losing her, I, along with my husband, David, and my son Matt, had received our full share. But only two and a half years later we buried her brother Gabriel, who was born with the same fatal metabolic disorder as his sister had and lived a mere 183 days.

I don't remember all the specifics of what our pastor said the two times we stood at the grave where Hope and Gabe are buried together, but I do remember that what he said really mattered. At Hope's graveside service, he said something like, "This is the place where we ask, 'Is the gospel really true?'" There was a deep *yes* inside me as he spoke, as I had been thinking about that question a lot in the months that led up to that difficult day. And I remember one specific verse he read that I was relieved to hear, because it, too, echoed my own desperation and discovery.

It is found in John 6, where John records that many of Jesus' followers had turned away and deserted him because some of his teachings were so hard for them to swallow. They were offended by what Jesus said, so they simply walked away from him. He didn't meet their immediate expectations, and he seemed to ask of them more than they wanted to give. They were far more interested in what they could get from Jesus than in getting more of Jesus. And when Jesus made it clear that what he wanted to give them was more of himself, they simply weren't interested any longer. At that point, as the throngs that had been following him began to slip away, Jesus turned to his twelve disciples and asked, "Are you also going to leave?"

I try to imagine the drama and emotion of that moment as Jesus said out loud what they were probably all thinking to themselves and as he called those closest to him to a decision. Simon Peter spoke up for the group, saying to Jesus, "Lord, to whom would we go? You have the words that give eternal life" (verse 68).

As my pastor read the Scripture, I could relate to those in the story who found some of Jesus' words difficult to understand and accept, and simply walked away. Perhaps you can too, as you have struggled to reconcile your understanding of what you've read about in the Bible, and your expectations of how God cares for those he loves, with your own difficult reality.

Jesus' question hung in the air, not only in that ancient setting, but also between him and me. "Are you also going to leave?" he asked. I could hear Jesus speaking to me, calling me to a commitment to trust him with this heartbreaking sorrow.

And I sensed the desperation and almost resignation in Peter's response to Jesus when he said, in essence, "Where else would we go? Who else could we turn to? You are the only one we can run to who has the power to give life just by speaking it into being." I remember thinking that my only hope for ever seeing Hope again was what the gospel tells us about how we find life that continues beyond the grave. Not having that hope to hold on to would have been an unbearable agony.

I also knew that Jesus provided my only hope for coming back to life myself, as I felt like the life in me was being snuffed out by sorrow.

In times of sorrow and disappointment, everything we believe can be called into question, can't it? Yet if we turn away from God, there really is no other place to go for meaning or peace. Anywhere away from him is hopelessly dark and empty.

I don't know what has brought sorrow into your life. Maybe you, too, have stood by a grave and said good-bye. Or maybe you have had to bury your dreams for a future with someone you love or your plans for doing something you have longed to do. Perhaps circumstances have forced you to leave behind a position you thought you were made for or come to terms with a frightening financial problem or a painful medical condition. Perhaps you live with ongoing sorrow over a child who has turned away from you or from faith. Maybe you are living with regret over the sorrow brought into your life by your own bad choices, or maybe you are living with resentment over the sorrow brought into your life by what someone else has done. Whatever the source of your sorrow, I wonder if you would be willing to spend a few quiet hours with me, listening to hear Jesus speak into it.

For Those Who Have Ears to Hear

Over the past ten years, I have found that Jesus has some significant things to say to those of us who hurt. But even as I write that, I'm afraid you might misunderstand me. I'm afraid you might think I'm going to go through the words of Jesus found in the Gospels to pick out only the parts that sound soothing or comforting to our modern ears. I'm not. I want to hear everything Jesus has to say to me, and I believe you do too. Just as I want to embrace his hopeful promise of "I am going . . . to prepare a place for you" (John 14:2, NIV), so also I want to accept his harder-to-hear promise that "here on earth you will have many trials and sorrows" (John 16:33). And just as I want to obey his instruction to "trust in God, and trust also in me" (John 14:1), so also I want to embrace his call to "love the LORD your God with all your heart, all your soul, and all your mind" (Matthew 22:37), which often seems like too tall an order for me.

We want the complete picture and deeper understanding that will bring clarity as well as comfort. We want to welcome needed correction and respond in repentance to uncomfortable conviction. Only the full truth can do that. We want to hear what Jesus is saying that brings solid hope we can grab hold of—even, and perhaps especially, in what he says that is hard to understand or just hard to hear.

When I tell you that we are going to listen carefully to words Jesus spoke, I'm also afraid you might think I'm suggesting that the words and teachings of Jesus have more authority or importance than other portions of the Bible. And I want to make sure you know that's not what I'm saying. We know that all Scripture is "God-breathed" (2 Timothy 3:16, NIV) and that Jesus himself gave all Scripture ultimate and equal authority (Matthew 5:17-18; Luke 16:17; John 10:35) as being the very Word of God. Jesus often responded to his detractors by saying, "Have you not read . . . ?" or "It is written . . ." making it clear that he considered Scripture to be the definitive authority.

Those of us who find ourselves in places of deep sorrow and suffering can find unique comfort and clarity in words of Jesus we might have skimmed over in the past, the ones we're so familiar with that they have little impact. We need to go beneath the surface to search for the deeper truths he is speaking to us and the implications of what he is saying. We recognize that we may have been hearing him speak through some filter that has warped, misapplied, or completely muffled what Jesus has said through his life and ministry, and we're open to having our perspectives completely reshaped.

That's what we will do in this book. We'll seek to have ears to hear in a fresh way eleven statements Jesus made. Honestly I've chosen many of these statements because they are the ones that have been most challenging for me to understand and apply to my own experiences. They are the ones that have caused me to say, "I just don't get it" as I read them and tried to fit them into my established understanding of the nature and purpose of the ministry of Jesus. I want to share them with you because over and over I find that the passages of Scripture that on the surface seem indiscernible to me hold some of the richest truths—life-changing, perspective-shaping, hope-giving truths.

I suppose this book is really the culmination of my search for deeper understanding that has come with the perspective of years and further study of the Scriptures since writing my earlier book *Holding On to Hope*. That book was written in the crucible of incredible circumstances—while I was pregnant with our son Gabriel—and published six months after he died. As I write now, many years down the road on this journey of sorrow, my thinking has not changed, but hopefully it has deepened and developed. I am still holding on to hope, but with an even firmer grip and clearer grasp of the nature of that hope.

Words of Real Comfort

Jesus said that we should listen closely to his words. "Pay close attention to what you hear," he said. "The closer you listen, the more understanding you will be given—and you will receive even more. To those who listen to my teaching, more understanding will be given. But for those who are not listening, even what little understanding they have will be taken away from them" (Mark 4:24-25).

And so I have to ask you, Do you want to listen closely to Jesus so that he will give you more understanding? Will you open your heart and mind to hear him speak into your sorrow? The words written on the pages of your Bible are not just detached religious dialogue that fails to intersect with your difficult reality. They are God's personal message to you.

The words Jesus speaks are far different from the words we speak. There is life, power, and authority in his every word. He speaks life into death, hope into despair, truth into delusion, meaning into futility, peace into panic. From his lips we receive wisdom, compassion, companionship, and so much more.

You may have found that most people around you simply don't know what to say to you about your sorrow and struggle. But I can assure you that Jesus knows just what to say to brokenhearted people. He knows just what we need to hear because he knows us better than we know ourselves. And Jesus understands the weight of our pain because he himself has plumbed the depths of suffering and sorrow. He experienced the sorrow that comes from the death of someone he loved dearly (Matthew 14:12-13; John 11:35-36) and the sorrow of knowing those he loves are hard hearted toward God (Luke 19:41). He suffered rejection and ridicule from his own family (John 7:5), homelessness (Matthew 8:20), temptation (Matthew 4:1-11), and of course, the cruel agony of the crucifixion (Matthew 27:32-44). Jesus has the resources of compassion and wisdom that no one else has. He is the one we need to hear from when our hearts have been broken by life in this world.

Fortunately Jesus is inclined to speak to us in our sorrow. He's not intimidated by awkwardness or hard questions. He is drawn to brokenhearted people. He knows we're not interested in pat answers or going through the motions of politeness, sentimentality, or religiosity. He knows we are desperately in need of the life and hope that come as we hear the truth.

So let's lean in to hear what Jesus has to say—out of his own brokenness into ours.

CHAPTER 1

HEAR JESUS SAYING,

I, Too, Have Known Overwhelming Sorrow

"My soul is crushed with grief to the point of death. Stay here and keep watch with me." MATTHEW 26:38

Jesus understands the crushing weight and agonizing loneliness of grief.

I've heard Jesus speaking to me about as long as I can remember.

When I was a little girl growing up in church, I heard Jesus, the Shepherd of lost sheep, calling me into the fold. I remember sitting in the pastor's office as a small child as he asked me if I understood what it meant to be lost. I pictured myself lost in the forest or the shopping mall. That's probably not exactly what he had in mind.

But the day came when I did understand it—at least to the extent a child can understand, since I wonder even now if I really understand how lost I truly was when Jesus found me and gave me the faith to trust him. I heard his voice clearly, calling me to himself, into the safety and contentment of his fold. Hearing his voice enabled me to say, "The LORD is my shepherd" (Psalm 23:1). He spoke life into a spiritually dead little eight-year-old girl, and I came alive to Jesus, the Savior of my soul.

But like many kids who grow up in the church and "make a decision for Christ" early in life, I came to a crisis point in my teens. I knew I had to decide if I would submit to the authority of Jesus in my life, not only on Sunday but throughout the week—and throughout my life. I heard Jesus telling me that being Savior of my soul meant being King of my heart. Oh, how I wanted to put him in charge yet so often doubted he could be trusted.

As I headed off to college and then began my career, Jesus, the Source of truth, began to shape my thinking, challenge my assumptions, prick my conscience, and expose my false beliefs. But rarely did he warm my heart or stir my passion. I found myself dry and disillusioned, so busy for him but often so far away from him. There were times I didn't know how to get the conversation going again, and I wasn't sure if he'd be willing to listen to me or if I even knew how to recognize his voice.

That's when, with a sense of desperation, I made a commitment to listening to him by reading and studying his Word day by day. Jesus, the Word of life, broke through my religious activity and accumulated Bible knowledge and began to convict me and change me. I fell in love with hearing his voice through his Word and developed an insatiable appetite for it—so much so that sometimes I wondered if he was preparing me for something.

Then I found out. The day came when I needed to hear the voice of Jesus in a way I had not heard it before. As I faced the heartbreak of losing my child, I needed to know that he understood the deep pain I was in. That's when I heard Jesus speak to me as the Man of Sorrows, as one who has suffered, as one who knows what it feels like to be crushed by grief to the point that it is squeezing the life out of you.

I heard Jesus speak to me as the Man of Sorrows, as one who has suffered, as one who knows what it feels like to be crushed by grief to the point that it is squeezing the life out of you.

So many of the other ways I had heard Jesus speaking to me—as the Shepherd of lost sheep, the Savior of my soul, the King of my heart, the Source of truth, and the Word of life—were mostly about listening for what he could do for me. But in this hard place of grief, hearing Jesus was less about what he could do for me and more about the companionship he could share with me. Jesus' words told me that he was safe to spend time with in my sadness.

I realized that my sorrow gave me the opportunity to know him with a depth I had not experienced before, in a way I could not have known him without going through deep sorrow myself.

Hearing Jesus, the Man of Sorrows, speak to me told me something about his character, his experience, his demeanor. It told me about his heart.

He has a heart that is broken.

Jesus, the Man of Sorrows, draws close to those of us who hurt and speaks to us as one whose heart has been broken too, calling us to himself.

Hear Jesus Convey His Own Deep Sorrow

A couple of years after my daughter died, during the days in which I was anticipating the birth of my son Gabriel, I read these words of Jesus, spoken in the garden of Gethsemane the night he was arrested.

> Jesus went with his disciples to a place called Gethsemane, and he said to them, "Sit here while I go over there and pray." He took Peter and the two sons of Zebedee along with him, and he began to be sorrowful and troubled. Then he said to them, "My soul is overwhelmed with sorrow to the point of death. Stay here and keep watch with me."
>
> MATTHEW 26:36-38, NIV

I made a note in my Bible that day in April 2001: "He understands how it feels to be 'overwhelmed with sorrow.'" What a

4

relief it was to know that Jesus understands what it is like to feel like sorrow is pressing the life out of you. He understands the lump in your throat, the heaviness in your chest, the sick feeling in your stomach.

His sorrow was so intense that he had a physical reaction to it. Luke writes that Jesus' perspiration became like "great drops of blood" (Luke 22:44). His agony was so intense that his blood burst through the capillaries and ruptured them, coloring the perspiration and enlarging the drops that continually fell to the ground.

Sometimes, in the desperation of deep grief, we begin to think that no one around us "gets it." We think that no one has ever hurt like we are hurting, that no one really understands how hard the simplest things of life are these days.

But Jesus does. Jesus is not a distant deity who knows nothing about the pain of disappointment and death. He knows firsthand. He understands. Hebrews 2:18 says, "Since he himself has gone through suffering and testing, he is able to help us when we are being tested."

Hear the words of Jesus: "My soul is overwhelmed with sorrow to the point of death," and let them draw you closer to him.

Have you always wanted to be closer to Jesus? I know you wouldn't have chosen this method to get there. We wish we could get closer to Jesus by saying a prayer, going to a Bible study, reading a book, or in some other convenient and controllable way. But the truth is, it's uniquely through our own sorrow that we can draw close to the Man of Sorrows.

It's in our suffering that we can truly begin to identify with his. We can finally get a tiny taste of what he was willing to endure out of his love for us. This is the deep knowing most of us have at least said we wanted, though we never thought it would cost us this much.

He has been here before us and has things about himself to reveal to us in this hard place, which we could not have been ready to listen for and learn without the hurt.

It is the kind of knowing Paul wanted when he said, "I want to know Christ and experience the mighty power that raised him from the dead. I want to suffer with him, sharing in his death, so that one way or another I will experience the resurrection from the dead!" (Philippians 3:10-11). Paul recognized that all his suffering—being imprisoned, shipwrecked, stoned, threatened, rejected, criticized, cold, and hungry—allowed him to experience a special fellowship with Jesus. It gave him access into a sacred fellowship—the fellowship of people who share in the sufferings of Jesus.

When we hear Jesus speaking into our sorrow, we hear his assurance that he has been here before us and that he has things about himself to reveal to us in this hard place, which we could not have been ready to listen for and learn without the hurt.

We hear his promise to walk with us on this difficult journey, providing companionship and compassion.

Hear Jesus Express His Aching Loneliness

When we listen closely to the words Jesus uttered in agony in the garden, we discover that it is not only the pain of our sorrow Jesus can relate to. He also understands the loneliness of it. He knows what it feels like to be at the lowest point of life and find that some of those you thought would be there are not there for you.

Here was Jesus, with his face to the ground, praying and asking God to take away the agonizing punishment for sin that was about to be poured out on him. Jesus, who had never committed any sin, was about to *become* sin.

Even though it had been his plan since the foundation of the world to give himself as a sacrifice for sin, Jesus was now standing at the precipice, staring into the cavernous darkness of death itself. And he was alone. Desperately alone.

Wrung out from the intensity of his pleading with God, he found his closest friends not praying as he had asked them to do but sleeping, seemingly oblivious to the battle going on inside his body and soul.

Lean in and listen to what Jesus says. Try to hear his tone of voice.

> *Couldn't you watch with me even one hour?*
> MATTHEW 26:40

Do you hear the humanness in his words? The aloneness?

On top of the betrayal Jesus was aching over, the humiliation he was anticipating, and the physical exhaustion he was enduring, Jesus was experiencing the loneliness of having friends who were not there for him when he needed them most.

Were there friends you thought would be there for you when the going got tough? And have you found that some of those friends have disappeared? They don't get it. They can't deal with it. They want you to get over it.

Find comfort in the companionship of the one who understands what it is like to be all alone. "He was despised and rejected—a man of sorrows, acquainted with deepest grief. We turned our backs on him and looked the other way. He was despised, and we did not care" (Isaiah 53:3).

When you feel like no one understands, listen to the words of Jesus and find comfort. He has been there.

When you feel like everyone has abandoned you and no one cares about the agony in your soul, listen to the words of Jesus and find companionship. Hear him calling you to a deeper, more real relationship with him than you've ever had before.

He, too, has been overwhelmed with sorrow. He will meet you in this place of pain and speak to you, letting you know that you are never alone.

As He Reminds You He Is with You

——————— ✿ ———————

I KNOW THIS SITUATION you're going through can cause you
to wonder if God, our Father, has abandoned you, if he has
left you alone. But you can be confident that he will never turn
away from you or leave you on your own. Anything and everything that could come between you and the Father was placed
on me when I hung on the cross. It was then that he turned
away from me—but only so he would never have to turn away
from you. He abandoned me that day so he could open his
arms to you forever. And he will never let you go.

Even though you may sometimes *feel* like you are on your
own, your feelings don't tell the whole story. You are not on
your own. I am with you always—in every situation and in
every moment. In your darkest, lowest experience, I am right
beside you. When everyone else falls away, I will still be here.
So you don't have to be afraid.

My Holy Spirit is with you and within you. He is the one
who helps you hear my voice and understand it. He is the
Counselor, showing you what is true and what is false so that
you can embrace the truth of who I am and what I'm holding out to you. He is the Advocate who turns the words on
the pages of your Bible into something powerful and personal
that can penetrate your soul and change your heart. He is the
Comforter who soothes your troubled thoughts with whispers
of my love for you.

Whenever you feel alone, remember that I came to make my

home with you. I'm here with you, even now, and I will never leave you.

Adapted from Mark 15:33-34; Matthew 28:20; Mark 6:50; John 16:13-15; John 14:16-26; John 1:14

CHAPTER 2

HEAR JESUS SAYING,

I, Too, Have Heard God Tell Me No

"My Father! If it is possible, let this cup of suffering be taken away from me. Yet I want your will to be done, not mine." MATTHEW 26:39

Jesus shows us what to do when God
doesn't give us what we want.

During the six months we had Hope, a number of people gave us books to read. One of the first was from a nurse in the hospital, given to me before we took Hope home. It was written by a woman whose child had drowned. I voraciously read it in our hospital room, seeking to gain insight into what might be ahead for us in grieving the loss of a child. I also bought a few books myself—some theological, some practical, and some with stories of loss I could relate to. In the aching quiet in the week after Hope died, I pulled out the unread stack and began to work my way through some of them, underlining parts that were especially meaningful to me. I remember coming upon a statement in one of them that said God was sad with me, and I wasn't sure what to make of that. It seemed like a nice idea, somewhat sentimental, perhaps intended to help me not to be mad at God. But I had a hard time believing it was true. I wondered how God could truly be sad with me since it had been in his power to cause things to work out differently.

Hearing what Jesus said to God when God did not answer his request the way he wanted helps us find our way forward when we hear God tell us no.

I think this is the wall that those of us who believe in God's sovereignty run into eventually. And when we feel its full force, it hurts. We think, *God, if you are powerful enough to have done things differently, why didn't you? How can I accept your comfort and believe you want to heal my broken heart when you could have kept me from experiencing this sorrow in the first place? If you'd only given me what I wanted, neither of us would have to be sad.*

It is at this place of inner conflict—where what we want and believe would be best seems to be at cross-purposes with the plans of God—where we need to hear Jesus speak. And we can hear him if we listen. Because Jesus ran into this same wall when what he wanted came in conflict with what God wanted. Hearing what Jesus said to God when God did not answer his request the way he wanted helps us find our way forward when we hear God tell us no.

Hear the Desperate Cries of Jesus

In the lowest part of my grief, as I was struggling to harmonize the power of God with the compassion of God, I came across these verses, and it was like a doorway opened up where I had hit a wall:

> *While Jesus was here on earth, he offered prayers*
> *and pleadings, with a loud cry and tears, to the*
> *one who could rescue him from death. And God*
> *heard his prayers because of his deep reverence for*
> *God. Even though Jesus was God's Son, he learned*
> *obedience from the things he suffered. In this way,*
> *God qualified him as a perfect High Priest, and he*
> *became the source of eternal salvation for all those*
> *who obey him.*
>
> HEBREWS 5:7-9

This passage helped me in several significant ways. First, when I read that Jesus offered up prayers with "a loud cry and tears," I could relate to that. I had so many tears that needed to come out. And it helped me to know that Jesus understands what that feels like—that he, too, has felt the sense of frustration and desperation that erupts in an agonizing groan. It helped me to know that Jesus doesn't dismiss suffering and sorrow by suggesting that it doesn't matter or that it shouldn't hurt. He, too, has cried hot tears.

The night before he was crucified, we hear Jesus crying out

to "the one who could rescue him from death"—the one who has the power to do things differently, to make another plan, to come up with another way. And that is the God I have cried out to—the God who is big enough and powerful enough to put the stars in place and orchestrate human history, the same God who is my Father and who loves me, the God who, it seemed to me, could have given my children healthy bodies rather than the flawed ones they were born with.

Reading these verses in Hebrews 5 drew me to look more closely and listen more carefully to the prayer of Jesus in Gethsemane as he faced the Cross. I needed to hear his struggle, which let me know I was not alone. But even more, I needed to hear his surrender, which pointed me toward the path of surrender that I wanted, deep down, to follow.

Hear Jesus Struggle with the Plan of God

In the Gospels, on the night Jesus was arrested, we find him pouring out his desire unashamedly before his Father as he prayed in the garden of Gethsemane. He was telling God what he wanted. And what he wanted was for there to be some other way of satisfying the justice of God besides offering himself as a sacrifice for sin. He did not want to have to experience the separation from his Father that becoming sin would demand if there were any other way.

There he was, at the precipice of the very purpose for which he had left heaven and become human. He had been telling his disciples that he was going to go to Jerusalem and that he would be arrested and crucified. Luke says, "Jesus resolutely set out for Jerusalem" (Luke 9:51). Jesus was determined not just to go to Jerusalem but to go to the cross. Earlier that week he had said, "Now my soul is deeply troubled. Should I pray, 'Father, save me from this hour'? But this is the very reason I came!" (John 12:27).

Jesus didn't go to the cross only because he had to. Obviously it was also what he wanted to do—at least in the big picture of things. And I think I understand that. In the big picture I want to obey God too. I want him to have his way in my life because I believe he knows what is best for me. But it is in the specifics where my desires threaten to take me in another direction. At these painful places in my life, I can't help but look up to God and ask, "Couldn't there be another way? Does obeying you really have to cost this much?"

That is what Jesus was asking in the garden as he stared into the white-hot anger God has toward sin that was about to envelop him. There was a battle going on, the most significant spiritual battle of all time. Satan was tempting Jesus to succumb to what he wanted in his flesh—to avoid the Cross—rather than embrace what he wanted deeply in his soul—to obey his Father and accomplish the work he came to do.

Satan was doing here what he always does. It's what he did in the Garden of Eden when he came to Adam and Eve and said, in essence, "If God really loved you, he wouldn't withhold something good from you" (Genesis 3). It's what Satan said to Jesus in the wilderness when he suggested that Jesus turn stones into bread rather than deny himself food. And it's essentially what he was saying to Jesus in the garden of Gethsemane: "If your Father really loved you, he wouldn't ask you to do this."

Jesus was perfectly holy, yet he didn't want to face the Cross if there was some other way—any other way. The Puritan theologian John Owen describes it this way in his commentary on Hebrews: "Christ would not have been human if he had not experienced extreme aversion to the things that were about to happen to him. . . . Although, by nature, he desired deliverance, since he was human, yet he did not desire this absolutely, as he was wholly given over to God's will."

It helps me to know that Jesus wrestled with God's plan for his life—and his death—even as he submitted to it, because I have wrestled with God's plan for my life even as I have sought to submit to it.

In sinless perfection, Jesus poured out the longings of his heart before his Father, without apology. We hear him cry out to his Father, asking if there could be another way, any way at all, to avoid this. A second time, then again a third, he pleaded for an alternative to the horror of abandonment by his Father. If such an alternative existed, wouldn't the Father provide it? But the obedient

Son's plea to his loving Father was met with silence—a tacit no from God.

It would seem to me that if anybody ever deserved to have his prayers answered in the affirmative, it was Jesus. Here he was in the garden of Gethsemane, pouring out his repeated request to his Father, asking him to accomplish the salvation of sinners in some other way. Yet God, through his silence, said no.

Jesus knows what it feels like to bring a heartfelt, passionate prayer to God and to hear God say, in effect, "I've got something else in mind. I have another plan. And that plan is going to require intense suffering on your part."

Somehow it helps me to know that Jesus wrestled with God's plan for his life—and his death—even as he submitted to it, because I, too, have wrestled with God's plan for my life even as I have sought to submit to it. Maybe you have too.

Hear Jesus Submit to the Purposes of God

Even though Jesus was struggling as he told God what he wanted, he was resolute about what he wanted most of all. Jesus said, "I want your will to be done, not mine" (Matthew 26:39).

Jesus didn't say this with a spirit of stoicism, fatalism, or martyrdom. He said it with a spirit of submission. He was able to submit what he wanted to what he wanted more. He had a greater longing that trumped and trampled his desire to avoid enduring the judgment of God. And that was to fulfill the purpose and plan of God—a desire kindled by his confidence in God's character and set aflame by his experience of God's love.

So he gave himself over to the goodness of God. Peter writes that when Jesus submitted himself to the Cross, he "left his case in the hands of God" (1 Peter 2:23). Jesus' confidence in the perfect plan and purposes of God put his own desires into proper perspective. And this is the perspective that you and I need to discipline our own fleshly desires. We need our confidence in God's goodness and justice to loom so large that we, too, can entrust ourselves to our Father without fear and without resentment.

We don't want to become hard and resentful toward God when he tells us no. We want to stay soft toward him, confident that if our loving Father has told us no, it is not because he is punishing us or being cruel to us. He is, in fact, loving us and doing what is best for us.

When we hear Jesus saying to his Father, "I want your will to be done, not mine," Jesus is speaking to us about the joy of surrender. He's showing us that he has walked this road before us. He, too, has been tempted to live by his own wants, and he knows what it takes to subdue those wants with the truth of God's promises, so that they do not win the battle.

Here is the hope we find in hearing Jesus speak into our own sorrowful situation: it is possible to overcome our own wants, to push through them to surrender. We see that as we pour our wants out before God, he gives us the grace we need to face whatever comes. We, too, can learn obedience from what we suffer. Our suffering does not have to be wasted pain. It can take us closer to the heartbeat of God as we pursue obedience in the hard places of life.

As we stop fighting and start welcoming his Holy Spirit, we discover that he is actually changing what we want. We begin to enjoy an inner strength and rest, a firm confidence that whatever God asks us to endure is purposeful. We begin to truly believe that the joy of surrendering to his will is going to be worth whatever it may cost.

What we need most is not to hear God say yes to our requests. What we need is to be filled with such deep confidence in the character of our Father that when he says no, we know he is doing what is right and good for us. What we need most is the faith to trust him.

Some claim that strong faith is defined by throwing our energies into begging God for a miracle that will take away our suffering and then believing without doubting that he will do it. But faith is not measured by our ability to manipulate God to get what *we* want; it is measured by our willingness to submit to what *he* wants.

It takes great faith to say to God, "Even if you don't heal me or the one I love, even if you don't change my circumstances, even if you don't restore this relationship, even if you allow me to lose what is most precious to me, I will still love you and obey you and believe that you are good. And I believe that you, as my loving Father, will use everything in my life—even the hard and hurtful things—for my ultimate good and your eternal glory, because you love me."

As we bring our wants and pour them out before our Father, he gives us the courage we need to surrender, so we can say along with Jesus, "I want your will to be done, not mine."

And he gives us the grace we need to say it—not through gritted teeth, but with open hands.

As He Prays for You

JUST AS I PRAYED for you when I was on earth, I am interceding for you before the throne of God, now and forever. In your utter weakness and deepest despair, when you don't have the words or the will to ask for what you need, my Holy Spirit is praying for you with the kind of passionate groaning for which there are no words.

You can be confident that God will say yes to what the Spirit prays for you, because he always pleads for God to accomplish his perfect will in your life. He is at work in you and on your behalf, tearing down the walls of your resistance to God's will.

The answer to the Spirit's prayers may not be what you would ask for on your own, but don't you want our Father's will to be done in your life more than you want to get what you want? Remember that he will cause everything in your life to work together for your ultimate good.

I hear your prayers, asking for your path to be smooth and asking the Father to bless your plans with success. But I have to tell you, that is not how I am praying for you. I love you too much for that. I am praying that when your plans go awry and your efforts fail, your faith will not. I am asking the Father to give you the good gift you have asked him for—more of my Holy Spirit at work in the interior of your life and character.

I am praying that you will walk in the truth and complete the work that has been entrusted to you—not so you can revel in the glory, but so you can experience the joy of giving the glory back to me. I am praying that the truth of my Word will teach you and refine you, even though that refining may be painful, because I know your greatest happiness will come as you become holy as I am holy.

The day is coming when you will see and share in the glory I have shared with my Father since before Creation. I'm praying that God will purify you and protect you until that coming day.

Adapted from Hebrews 7:25; Romans 8:26-28; Luke 22:31-32; 11:13; John 17; 1 Peter 1:16; 2 John 1:4; Hebrews 13:21; John 14:3; Philippians 1:6

CHAPTER 3

HEAR JESUS SAYING,
I Am Willing to Heal Your Deadliest Disease

"I am willing. . . . Be healed!" MARK 1:41

Jesus knows what we need most of all.

David and I were seated next to a prominent pastor and his aide at a formal dinner as we began to work our way through the salad course and introductions around the table. There were books in the middle of the tables by various authors in attendance, and the pastor picked up my book and asked me what it was about.

That is always a hard question to answer briefly and simply because it leads to the story of Hope's and Gabriel's lives and deaths. When we came to a natural stopping point in the story, the pastor, without missing a beat, began to tell us about a couple in his church whose child had been diagnosed with significant physical problems. "That couple really prayed, and their child was miraculously healed," he told us before turning his attention back to his steak.

It was kind of hard to know how to respond. Of course, we were thrilled that the child's health had been restored. But it felt to David and me that hanging in the air around the table was a suggestion that if we had prayed more or if we had prayed more earnestly or if we had had more faith, perhaps our children would not have died.

Many times before and since, we've had conversations with those who seem to suggest that miraculous physical healing is out there for any and all who have adequate faith to tap into it.

Those of us who do not get the physical healing we prayed for can be left assuming that either our faith is deficient or God is unable or unwilling to heal us or the one we love. And in some ways, a surface-level tour through the Gospels can add to that assumption. Over and over we see Jesus healing people of their physical diseases, so we can't help but wonder if he will do the same for us, too.

Certainly the leper who came to Jesus wondered if he would be a recipient of the healing touch of Jesus. His disease probably started with just a few painful spots. Then the spots went numb. Slowly his body became a mass of ulcerated growths. The skin around his eyes and ears began to bunch; he lost his fingers and toes to unnoticed and untreated injuries. His eyebrows and eyelashes fell out, and his hair turned white. His rotting flesh gave off an unbearable odor. To be a leper in Jesus' day was to have no future and no hope, to know only ongoing deterioration, disfigurement, and despair.

Lepers were forbidden to come anywhere near non-lepers because of the deep fear of contagion, as well as cultural laws quarantining them from the rest of society. So this man must have had a deep sense of desperation to risk coming anywhere near Jesus. Or perhaps he was emboldened to approach Jesus because he sensed in him not only healing power but also a heart that was tender toward those who hurt.

> *A man with leprosy came and knelt in front of Jesus,*
> *begging to be healed. "If you are willing, you can heal*
> *me and make me clean," he said.*
>
> MARK 1:40

He didn't really ask Jesus directly for healing. It's almost as if he didn't want to be presumptuous. He knew Jesus could heal him if he wanted to. He just didn't know if Jesus wanted to.

And I can relate to that. Maybe you can too.

It is what Jesus did in this interaction that is, perhaps, more shocking than what he said.

> *Moved with compassion, Jesus reached out and*
> *touched him.*
>
> MARK 1:41

This lonely leper must have been longing for years to feel the loving touch of another human being. No one besides other lepers ever touched him anymore; it was considered too dangerous, completely taboo. But Jesus, feeling deep inside himself the pain this leper felt day after difficult day, reached out and touched him.

Certainly Jesus could have healed the leper without touching him. Jesus healed people just by speaking that healing into being many times. But Jesus reached out and touched this man most people avoided.

> *"I am willing," he said. "Be healed!" Instantly the leprosy disappeared, and the man was healed.*
> MARK 1:41-42

Jesus, Are You Willing?

I still get a lump in my throat when I read the words Jesus spoke to this leper who came to him for healing because it reminds me of when I came upon this story in the months after Hope died. In my sadness, I read this verse and heard Jesus saying to the leper, "I am willing." But I also heard what seemed to be its echo in my own ears—Jesus saying to me, "I was not willing." It hurt my feelings as I pictured Jesus refusing me my miracle of healing for my daughter. I felt like this was a party I wasn't invited to or a privilege that wasn't extended to me.

But even as I felt the sting of presumed refusal, I knew something had to be wrong with that picture. I knew I had to figure out what Jesus was really saying through this account of the leper and the many other healing miracles I'd read about in the Gospels. I knew that if I could come to a clearer understanding of what Jesus was saying through them, it would help me understand what to expect from him here and now.

So I began to read about and compare the miracles of Jesus' ministry, considering the role faith played in each one, noting the different methods Jesus used to heal, and looking for the lesson or purpose he seemed to have in each healing.

First, it became obvious to me that Jesus didn't heal everyone of everything. As he began to heal many in the multitudes who came to him for physical healing, the word began to get around, and many who were sick came to him looking for their miracle. But while he healed multitudes of people, Jesus didn't always heal everyone who came to him.

It seems to me that if Jesus' ministry was mostly about healing physical sickness, he would have healed more pervasively and perhaps even more permanently. But we know that every person who was physically healed by Jesus during his earthly ministry eventually died. At some point their bodies gave out when some other sickness or simply old age overruled the earlier miracles.

When we look at the healing miracles of Jesus, we see that some of the people he healed knew and believed in who he was. Others didn't. While faith was always present, it wasn't always the faith of the one who was healed. Sometimes it was faith expressed by someone in authority over that person or in relationship with that person, as with the healing of the Roman officer's servant (Matthew 8:5-13) and Jairus's daughter (Luke 8:49-55).

The other thing I noticed in the numerous accounts of healings in the Gospels was that the Bible often says Jesus was moved by compassion (Matthew 14:14; Mark 1:41; and Luke 7:13-14). Whatever else Jesus' healing ministry was about, it became obvious to me that he is moved by the physical suffering we experience. He is responsive to our pain. He hurts when we hurt.

But it was the insight I found in the Gospel of John that especially helped me, where John states clearly the reason Jesus performed healing miracles and other kinds of miracles as well:

> *The disciples saw Jesus do many other miraculous*
> *signs in addition to the ones recorded in this book.*
> *But these are written so that you may continue to*
> *believe that Jesus is the Messiah, the Son of God, and*
> *that by believing in him you will have life by the*
> *power of his name.*
>
> JOHN 20:30-31

While the miracles Jesus performed reveal his love and compassion for hurting people, the greater purpose of each miracle was to draw people into a deeper spiritual reality, a greater understanding of him that will give us the life we're so desperate for. We see here that Jesus really does want us to live. He came and he healed in order to show us there's a deeper sickness than physical blindness, paralysis, or fever that he has the power to heal. This sickness set in long before, on what must have been God's saddest day.

God's Saddest Day

Recently I was walking with some friends in the park near my home on a beautiful spring morning when we began to praise God with eyes wide open. As we expressed our gratitude for the wonder and beauty that surrounded us, we also acknowledged the brokenness that surrounds us—a brokenness that is as crushing as the beauty is breathtaking. And as we lifted up our prayers of praise to God, my friend Teri said something to God I had never thought of before. She spoke of what she described as his "saddest day."

Now if you had asked me prior to this what God's saddest day was, my response probably would have been to name the day of Jesus' crucifixion. When I think about the sky growing dark and the earth shaking at the hour of his death, it seems to me that all creation became an outlet for the intense sorrow of God as it poured over a guilty world.

But perhaps that was not God's saddest day. Perhaps his saddest day was when he went looking for Adam and Eve in the Garden, and they were hiding. That was the day when we as the human race grabbed hold of something outside of him in an attempt to find joy and satisfaction. We believed the lie that God was withholding something from us that would make us happy. And in our choice to seek satisfaction apart from him, a great cavern of separation came between us. No longer could we walk together with God without shame or pretense. No longer could we enjoy a life of fulfillment, free of frustration.

We opened the door to sin that day, and it came rushing into every aspect of our existence, taking away our freedom and our unfettered enjoyment of God himself. Into the purity of the world God created, sin brought a poison that penetrated everything. And into the relationship we enjoyed with God, sin built a barrier. We went from being at peace with God to feeling threatened by him. Guilt and fear took over where innocence and openness had once ruled.

What God had created and called good was invaded and infiltrated by the effects of evil. Surely God must have felt the weight of sorrow over what was lost—Paradise lost. Surely this must have been his saddest day, when we became sick with sin.

And yet, there was a glimmer of hope in the midst of the destruction. That same day God said to Satan, "I will cause hostility between you and the woman, and between your offspring and her offspring. He will strike your head, and you will strike his heel" (Genesis 3:15). God promised that someday he would send a hero who would fight Satan to the death. That hero would suffer, but he would win. Jesus, our hero, would defeat forever the power of sin to alienate us from God and inflict us with suffering.

The rest of the Bible is the story of God's fulfillment of this promise. Satan struck Christ's heel on the Cross, but the day is coming when Jesus will crush Satan's head. We read about that coming day in Revelation 22:

> *The angel showed me a river with the water of life, clear as crystal, flowing from the throne of God and of the Lamb. It flowed down the center of the main street. On each side of the river grew a tree of life, bearing twelve crops of fruit, with a fresh crop each month. The leaves were used for medicine to heal the nations. No longer will there be a curse upon anything. For the throne of God and of the Lamb will be there, and his servants will worship him.*
>
> REVELATION 22:1-3

There is a day coming when death and disease will be healed for good. That is our sure hope in the midst of sorrow.

But for now we live in an in-between time, in which suffering is an ongoing reality as we await the healing to come when Christ ushers in the new heaven and new earth. Paul describes the frustration we feel living in the here and now as we wait for that day:

> *We believers also groan, even though we have the Holy Spirit within us as a foretaste of future glory, for we*

long for our bodies to be released from sin and suffer-
ing. We, too, wait with eager hope for the day when
God will give us our full rights as his adopted chil-
dren, including the new bodies he has promised us.

ROMANS 8:23

What were Jesus' miracles all about? The healing miracles of Jesus in the Gospels give us a foretaste of what is coming because of the decisive blow Jesus dealt to the power of sin and death when he died on the cross. The day is coming when the healing ministry of Jesus will come to full fruition. His healing will be pervasive and plentiful . . . and it will be eternal.

Until then, we "wait with eager hope" for that day. We read the Gospels and see glimpses of Jesus' healing in the past. We also catch glimpses of it now in our own experiences. God can and does heal the sick today in answer to our prayers—but not always, and not everyone.

When we insist that God's promises of complete healing must be applied to our lives now as well as in the fullness that is to come, we're mistakenly expecting in this age what God has reserved for the next. God's primary purpose in the here and now is not to rid us of sickness and pain but to purify us and empower us to place all our hopes in his promises, trusting that one day they will become the reality we will know fully and enjoy forever.

Jesus Speaks to Our Most Significant Sickness

Jesus came to get to the real root of our problem, the cause of all our suffering and sorrow. He came on a mission to destroy what has brought on all our misery: sin. That's the deeper meaning to what he is saying to us when we hear him tell the leper, "I am willing. Be healed!"

The effects of leprosy on a person's body provide a vivid picture of the effects of sin on a person's soul. Just as it takes only one spot to indicate that a person's body is permeated with leprosy, it takes only one spot of sin in our lives to reveal that we have the spiritual disease of sin that has permeated our whole selves. Our thoughts, our emotions, and our wills have all become infected with sin. Like leprosy, sin infects the whole person, and it is ugly, loathsome, corruptive, contaminating, and alienating, and ultimately it leads to death.

When we insist that God's promises of complete healing must be applied to our lives now as well as in the fullness that is to come, we're mistakenly expecting in this age what God has reserved for the next.

So in reaching out to heal leprosy, Jesus was showing us that his touch can cure sin. In healing the leper, Jesus was saying to us, "I can heal you of the most destructive, deadly disease in your life—the disease of sin." In fact, every healing miracle of his earthly ministry points to Jesus' ability to heal our deeper spiritual sickness of sin.

When Jesus said to the blind man, "Go, for your faith has healed you" (Mark 10:52), he was saying that he can remove the spiritual ignorance that keeps us from seeing who he really is.

When Jesus said to the man who had been demon possessed, "Go home to your family, and tell them everything the Lord has done for you and how merciful he has been" (Mark 5:19), he was saying that he can free us from enslaving, dominating sin.

When Jesus said to the paralytic, "Be encouraged, my child! Your sins are forgiven" (Matthew 9:2), he was saying that he can take away the sin that cripples and incapacitates us.

When Jesus said to the woman who had hemorrhaged for twelve years, "Daughter, your faith has made you well. Go in peace. Your suffering is over" (Mark 5:34), he was saying that he can stop the waste of spiritual power and life that results from ongoing sin.

When Jesus said to the ears and mouth of the deaf and mute man, "Be opened" (Mark 7:34), he was saying that he can overcome our sin-induced inability or refusal to hear from God and speak for God.

When Jesus spoke into the tomb, "Lazarus, come out!" (John

11:43), he was saying that he brings back to life what sin has put to death, just by the power of his word.

When Jesus said, "I am willing. Be healed!" to the leper, he was saying that he wants to cleanse us from the pervasive sin that will prove eternally fatal without his healing touch.

And now I realize that Jesus turns toward me when I call out to him for healing. Now I can hear him lovingly responding to me, saying, "I am willing. Be healed." He is at work in my life, even now, bringing healing to the wounded places where sin has left its ugly mark. He certainly isn't finished yet, but I know the day is coming when his work in me will be complete.

I've also come to peace realizing that Jesus did not withhold his healing touch from Hope or Gabe. He has taken them to himself and will, at the resurrection, give them glorious bodies (Philippians 3:21). And this is no get-God-off-the-hook cop-out. Their healing was not second rate or second best. It is everything we would ask for and long for.

Jesus Willingly Takes Our Sickness on Himself

As we see Jesus reaching out to touch the leper, we recognize that no matter how infected and offensive we are because of the sin in our lives, nothing we are—within or without—can ever cause Jesus to withdraw from us or refuse to touch us. He is filled with compassion over how sin has hurt us and infected our lives with misery. So he reaches out to touch us in our utter guilt and helplessness, taking upon himself our sin-sickness and imparting to us his health and wholeness. This is what the prophet Isaiah foretold about the work of Christ:

> *He was pierced for our rebellion, crushed for our sins.*
> *He was beaten so we could be whole.*
>   *He was whipped so we could be healed.*
> *All of us, like sheep, have strayed away.*
>   *We have left God's paths to follow our own.*
> *Yet the LORD laid on him the sins of us all.*

ISAIAH 53:5-6

When Jesus reached out and touched the leper, he was showing us that he is willing to take our sin-sickness upon himself and in the process transfer to us his own healthy glow of righteousness and acceptance before God.

This freedom from sin is the miraculous healing that is beyond our understanding, and the too-good-to-be-true promise of the gospel—that when we come to him in repentance and faith, Jesus gives us his righteousness and takes our sin upon himself in a miraculous and mysterious exchange. It is not merely having faith that saves us. Our faith is a conduit by which this miraculous healing exchange takes place. When we come to Christ in faith, we are essentially saying, "I'm sick and I can't get well on my own. Jesus, I trust you and depend on you to make me acceptable to God."

Jesus wants to heal you. He wants to bring you into the complete wholeness he created you for, and if you have turned away from your old life as a slave to your sinful impulses and away from trying to be good enough on your own, and turned toward Jesus in utter dependence, he has already begun to do so. As you depend on him, he will continue to transform your sin-ridden life so that it will reflect more and more of his holiness and health.

As you read the Gospels, don't insist that God heal you here and now. Don't reduce the nature of his healing power and intentions. Jesus did not die on the cross to give you a certain number of days of health on this earth but to fit you, body and soul, for eternity in a new heaven and a new earth.

Perhaps what we need is not a miraculous healing of our bodies but a more powerful awareness of our sin-sickness.

When we feel disappointed by the spiritual nature of the fulfillment of God's promises to heal us, it reveals the truth about what we think about our sin. We don't really see our sin as that big of an issue. As we compare ourselves to those around us, we think we're pretty good. We think of our sin problem as more like a case of the sniffles than a terminal disease.

Our disappointment also reveals that we don't value the eternal promises of God as much as we want him to fix what we see as our most significant problems. What we really want from him is to give us everything he has promised us here and now. We think that physical life on this earth—the length of it and the quality of it—is of ultimate importance. We have a hard time grasping the signficance and the reality of the life to come.

Perhaps what we need is not a miraculous healing of our bodies but a more powerful awareness of our sin-sickness. We need to see our sin for the certain death it delivers—not just to our mortal bodies, but to our eternal souls. Only then can we appreciate the miracle Jesus offers us when he heals us of this fatal disease of sin.

You and I have a disease much more deadly than leprosy. While leprosy can destroy the body, sin kills the soul.

So we come to Jesus with our deadly disease of sin and say, "Lord, if you are willing, you can heal me." He turns no one away, no matter how disfigured by sin. Instead, he looks at us lovingly and says, "I am willing."

Of His Healing for You

————————— ✤ —————————

I AM JEHOVAH-ROPHI, the Lord who heals. Healing is not just something that I do; it is my very nature, reflected in my name. I am the source and sustainer of life itself. So in your sickness, look to me. I want to heal you.

And I mean really heal you—not just heal your body in a temporary way, but heal your spirit, soul, and body in a pervasive and permanent way. I want to bring you to the place of complete wholeness I created you for. My healing work has already begun in your life—it began when I first drew you to myself. The deeper you go in me and the longer you abide in me, the more healing you will experience.

It is my healing touch that soothes your ailing body, your aching heart, your troubled mind, and your weary soul. It is my touch that heals you from the self-absorption that consumes you, the apathy toward me that depletes you, the lust that brings you shame and regret, the materialism that leaves you unsatisfied, the unforgiveness that isolates you from others—all the sin that has made your soul so sick.

I know it is never comfortable when my Spirit shows you the areas of your life that are offensive to me. I'm not trying to hurt you by calling attention to your sin; I'm helping you. Won't you let me love you in this way? Just turn toward me and begin to confess those sins rather than ignoring them or trying to hide them. I won't turn away from you. I will cleanse you.

This repentance I'm calling you to is not a onetime thing.

I'm asking you to make it your way of life. As you live in brokenness before me, I will continue to show you the things in your life that keep you from closer fellowship with me—not to condemn you or discourage you, but to draw you into the full and free life I have for you.

On the cross, I dealt decisively with your deepest and most destructive disease, and even now you are being healed by my wounds. There I destroyed the power of sin to rule your life and determine your destiny.

I am not unmoved by the pain in your life. As you lay it before me and invite me into it, you will find me moving toward you, bringing you peace.

Adapted from Exodus 15:26; Acts 17:25; Hebrews 1:3; Romans 6:13; John 15:4, NKJV; Luke 6:19; Luke 5:31-32; Matthew 13:15; 1 John 1:9; Ephesians 5:26; Philippians 1:6; John 16:8; Colossians 3:5; 1 Peter 2:24

CHAPTER 4

HEAR JESUS SAYING,
I Will Save You from Yourself

---

*"You are seeing things merely from a human point
of view, not from God's."* MATTHEW 16:23

Jesus saves us from a wasted life of always
trying to get our own way.

David and I lead a class every Sunday following the worship
service at our church, in which our group simply discusses the
sermon. We've been doing it for about four years now, and it
is a highlight of our week to spend that time with our brothers
and sisters, seeking how we can understand and apply the truths
we've been exposed to. Our friend Hal Hadden calls our class
a place "where you can think out loud and hurt out loud." It is
a safe place to do both.

Recently our conversation came around to our expectations
of God and how we tend to question God's goodness in some
situations rather than allowing God to define what is good.

A member of the class recalled the Sunday seven years ago when David and I stood before the congregation. Our church family had walked with us through some difficult days, joining with us in making the most of Hope's brief life as they took her into their arms and into their hearts, and sharing the deep sorrow we felt in the emptiness following her death. So when we stood up to tell them that I was pregnant again despite the surgical steps we had taken to prevent another pregnancy, they could not hold back their joy. They burst out in applause before we could get it all out. But there was more to get out. After the applause began to die down, David added, "And this child will have the same fatal syndrome his sister, Hope, had."

There was an audible expression of dismay. This was not the happy ending everyone felt would have been the appropriate fit for our story, certainly not the one they felt would make following God look good.

Our friend in class told us that she wept that morning and into the next day. It didn't seem right to her. And it didn't fit her idea of the way we can expect our good God to work in the lives of believers. It seemed to her that the fitting end to the story would be that God would bless us with a healthy child, showing the watching world that he makes up for the losses he allows into our lives.

And she wasn't the only one.

When we shared our news that Sunday, we had known for about seven weeks that I was pregnant. But we had told only a handful of people while we waited to get the results from the prenatal testing that would indicate what was ahead for us—another healthy child like our son, Matt, or another child with Zellweger syndrome like our daughter, Hope.

It was interesting how several of the godly people we shared our secret with responded. I remember one friend who sternly instructed me not to be afraid but to believe that this child would be healthy, almost as if that confidence would have the power to make it so. Another said that God certainly would not give us another child with the syndrome—that "God is not like that and would not do that." Another friend told us she was certain this child would be healthy—as a reward for our faithfulness to God in the face of losing Hope. Even my ob-gyn told me he was sure this child would be healthy—based not on any medical examination or information but purely on his own compassionate desire and innate optimism.

Honestly I don't think their responses had much to do with theological introspection. They loved us. And they couldn't imagine us having to endure another devastating loss.

But I remember thinking that while we knew they wanted to be encouraging and positive, we were the ones who were going to have to live with the disillusionment if we grabbed hold of the uninformed expectation of a healthy baby. I guess we also recognized that they had no practical or scriptural foundation for such certainty. *God does not owe us,* I remember thinking. *Certainly many faithful followers experience more than one heartbreaking loss. Why would we think we are somehow above that?*

I thought about how believers throughout history, and even now in various parts of the world, experience loss after loss, not in spite of, but exactly because of their faithfulness to Jesus. The assumption that God should give faithful believers a comfortable life, and certainly no more than one dose of sorrow, seems to be an American-made version of the Christian life that doesn't hold up to examination. And it certainly doesn't hold up to what we see in the lives of followers of Jesus in the Bible. We've mistakenly determined an appropriate and acceptable trajectory of the victorious Christian life, thinking if we declare our solid belief in Jesus, he somehow owes us a life of limited difficulty.

> *Believers of other times, and even now in other parts of the world, experience loss after loss, not in spite of, but exactly because of, their faithfulness to Jesus.*

Our Assumptions about Discipleship

It seems that the apostle Peter had some misconceptions about discipleship himself early on. Peter had just had a powerful and pivotal conversation with Jesus, declaring his solid personal belief in Jesus as the Son of God. His interaction with Jesus is recorded in Matthew 16:

*When Jesus came to the region of Caesarea Philippi,
he asked his disciples, "Who do people say that the
Son of Man is?"*

*"Well," they replied, "some say John the Baptist,
some say Elijah, and others say Jeremiah or one of the
other prophets."*

Then he asked them, "But who do you say I am?"

*Simon Peter answered, "You are the Messiah, the
Son of the living God."*

*Jesus replied, "You are blessed, Simon son of John,
because my Father in heaven has revealed this to you.
You did not learn this from any human being. Now
I say to you that you are Peter (which means 'rock'),
and upon this rock I will build my church, and all
the powers of hell will not conquer it. And I will give
you the keys of the Kingdom of Heaven. Whatever
you forbid on earth will be forbidden in heaven, and
whatever you permit on earth will be permitted in
heaven."*

MATTHEW 16:13-19

Jesus said to Peter, "You are blessed. . . . I will give you the
keys of the Kingdom." Pretty heady stuff, I'd imagine—hearing
Jesus speak words of victory and blessing and power. Peter must
have been inspired to want to press onward and upward to take
the hill ahead of them.

But then Jesus said something that seemed to put it all in jeopardy, at least in terms of the way Peter must have assumed his future would take shape.

> *From then on Jesus began to tell his disciples plainly that it was necessary for him to go to Jerusalem, and that he would suffer many terrible things at the hands of the elders, the leading priests, and the teachers of religious law. He would be killed, but on the third day he would be raised from the dead.*
>
> MATTHEW 16:21

First Jesus said the powers of hell would not be able to defeat them, and then he said that it was necessary for him to go to Jerusalem, where he would suffer unjustly, be killed, and then be raised from the dead. It just didn't make sense to Peter.

Peter had come to see Jesus as the fulfillment of all the prophecies that spoke of a conquering Messiah who would rule the world in peace and justice. But he had not yet put it together that the victorious Savior was the same person Isaiah described as the suffering Servant. Looking into the future, Peter saw God's Kingdom in terms of reigning and ruling, not ridicule and rejection.

And like us, Peter liked the sound of blessing, building, and overcoming. Submitting and suffering didn't fit into his designs for his future.

> *Peter took [Jesus] aside and began to reprimand him*
> *for saying such things. "Heaven forbid, Lord," he*
> *said. "This will never happen to you!"*
>
> MATTHEW 16:22

Imagine being so bold and brash as to reprimand Jesus! And yet don't we see ourselves in this exchange? Can't we hear in Peter's confrontation our own frustration with the plans God sometimes lays out for us? Haven't we been confident that our painful circumstances couldn't possibly be the plan of God for us?

Here is where we need to hear Jesus speaking into our sorrow. But it hurts a bit to hear it.

> *Jesus turned to Peter and said, "Get away from me,*
> *Satan! You are a dangerous trap to me. You are*
> *seeing things merely from a human point of view,*
> *not from God's."*
>
> MATTHEW 16:23

One minute Peter was hailed as the foundation of the church. The next minute he was branded as a tool of Satan. One minute Jesus said Peter was speaking the revelation of God. The next minute Jesus scolded Peter for speaking the foolishness of a mere man.

I'm not sure what Peter's thought process was in that moment. We do know that Peter and the others were jockeying for position in the earthly kingdom they expected Jesus to usher in. So maybe Peter's outburst was prompted by seeing all those dreams of grandeur turn into an unimaginable nightmare.

But I don't think that was all it was. I think Peter loved Jesus. And I think he could not bear the thought that the Jesus he loved so dearly would be killed like a common criminal. *Surely,* Peter must have thought, *God's plan for your life could not include a cross.*

I think perhaps it was the same thing that caused godly people in our lives to tell us they were sure God would not give us another child who would die. They loved us. And they couldn't imagine we would once again have to walk through the suffering we had walked through over the previous two years. *Surely,* they must have thought, *God's plan for your lives could not include a cross.*

How quickly we get off track when we refuse to embrace God's method of overcoming, when we refuse his call to follow him to the Cross. You see, when Jesus spoke, he was responding to Peter's Satan-inspired suggestion that Jesus should not have to go to the Cross, that victory could be won through strength instead of weakness, military might rather than selfless surrender, political positioning rather than sacrificial submission, personal charisma rather than authentic humility.

Jesus knew that the way of victory is always and only by dying to doing things the way that makes sense on merely human terms. The way of Jesus is paradox. On the surface of things, we have a hard time making sense of it. But deep down, we know it is true.

The Paradox That Helps Us Let Go

Jesus said to his disciples,

> *If any of you wants to be my follower, you must turn*
> *from your selfish ways, take up your cross, and follow*
> *me. If you try to hang on to your life, you will lose*
> *it. But if you give up your life for my sake, you will*
> *save it.*

MATTHEW 16:24-25

The disciples knew well what Jesus was alluding to when he said, "Take up your cross." They had seen many a condemned criminal being compelled to carry the instrument of his suffering and death as he stumbled toward his own execution.

We want to say to Jesus on their behalf and our own, "Surely God's plan for my life doesn't have to include a cross!" But we know that God's plan for some of the disciples did include a literal cross. According to Christian tradition, four of the twelve were martyred through crucifixion. Peter was one of them, although tradition tells us that he insisted on being crucified upside down because he didn't feel worthy of dying in the same way as his beloved Jesus.

But for most of Jesus' disciples—including you and me—it is unlikely that we will be called upon to take up a literal cross made of wood. More likely, we will be invited to willingly take up an uncomfortable method of putting our wills and wants, our plans and preferences, our desires and demands to death. Jesus was establishing a pattern for everyone who dares to identify himself or herself as one of his followers. Self-denial is at the heart of what it means to follow him.

We will be invited to willingly take up an uncomfortable method of putting our wills and wants, our plans and preferences, our desires and demands to death.

What happens if we really hear Jesus speaking these words of self-denial into our sorrow? Our thinking will no longer be confined to a merely human point of view. We will begin to think like Jesus. The reason I know this is possible is because that's what happened to Peter. More than thirty years after Peter was rebuked by Jesus, he wrote the following in a letter to fellow disciples of Jesus around the world:

> *Since Jesus went through everything you're going through and more, learn to think like him. Think of your sufferings as a weaning from that old sinful habit of always expecting to get your own way. Then you'll be able to live out your days free to pursue what God wants instead of being tyrannized by what you want.*
>
> I PETER 4:1-2, *The Message*

"Learn to think like him," Peter wrote. Peter took to heart the rebuke of Jesus and became an evangelist for embracing the way Jesus thinks about suffering. Peter was no longer bent toward advancing God's Kingdom in the world through power and victory. He finally recognized that the Kingdom of God advances in this world and in our lives as we put to death our demands to live life our way.

Do you hear Jesus speaking, perhaps rebuking you for thinking about the losses in your life from a merely human perspective? Are you willing to count the cost of what it will mean to follow him, to think like him about suffering? Jesus is up front about what it will cost to follow him. It will cost us everything.

To follow Jesus is to follow a crucified Jesus who invites us to share in his suffering. It requires that we say no to the demands of our sinful flesh and that we refuse to succumb to Satan's suggestion that we insist on having what we think will make us truly happy.

Ultimately, dying to ourselves is the only way to really live. Jesus saves us from wasting our lives by trying to save them. Jesus lovingly saves us from ourselves.

As He Invites You to Follow Him

FOLLOW ME. When I say these two words to you, I'm offering you an invitation. But I must also tell you that I'm issuing you a command. Following me cannot be a halfhearted pursuit. If there's anything keeping you from following me, you must get rid of it.

Follow me. It will require that you stop following the ways of this world. You can't value what the world values or love what the world loves, because the world does not value me or love me. But if you follow me, I will lead you away from a life of chasing after possessions and experiences and passions that will never end up satisfying you.

Follow me. But you should know that following me means going to my Cross. Following me requires a death to your self-worship so that I can live in you and through you. You will live in your earthly body not by taking care of yourself but by trusting in me.

Follow me. I will save you from the tyranny of always thinking about yourself first and foremost—your needs, your discomforts, your hurts, your wants, your preferences, your rights. Instead, I'll show you how to surrender your demands for the life you think you deserve so you'll want, most of all, to please me.

Follow me, not into a life of comfort, but into a life of significance. Following me may cost you your very life, but you can be confident that I will more than make up for everything you lose along the way. And in the process, your life will witness to the world that you treasure me more than anything and everything you've let go of.

Follow me, listening for the sound of my voice in your life. I know there are plenty of voices all around you and even inside you telling you what to think and what to believe and how to live. Don't let those voices drown out my voice in your ear. Tune in to my voice by opening up my Word. Judge every other voice by its harmony with mine.

Follow me to where I am going. I am going to prepare a place for you. When everything is ready, I will come and get you, so that you will always be with me where I am.

Adapted from John 12:26; Matthew 16:24; Galatians 2:20; 1 Peter 2:21; Matthew 13:44; Luke 9:61-62; 1 Peter 4:1-2; Hebrews 1:1-2; John 10:27; 14:2-3

CHAPTER 5

HEAR JESUS SAYING,

I Will Keep You Safe

"Don't be afraid of those who want to kill you. They can only kill your body; they cannot touch your soul." MATTHEW 10:28

Jesus protects us from eternal harm.

It was one of those perfect evenings spent having dinner on our back patio, eating salmon off the grill and talking late into the night with friends we hadn't connected with in a long time. Since the last time we were together, our friend Jenny had been in an all-out battle against a vicious form of cancer, and we wanted to hear the whole story.

She told us about her experience of meeting with a radiologist about the treatment that had been recommended to her. With seemingly no sensitivity, and offering no caveats of reassurance, he told her that the process was going to be the most painful thing she would ever experience, explaining that her skin in the affected area would burn off and peel away.

"But the Bible says, 'When you pass through the waters, I will be with you; and when you pass through the rivers, they will not sweep over you. When you walk through the fire, you will not be burned,'" she said to him (Isaiah 43:2, NIV).

He replied, "Do you really believe that stuff?"

"Yes," she said. "I do."

Needless to say, she found someone else to administer the treatments.

But the radiologist had been right about the intensity of the pain and the burning. Her skin burned away, and it was so excruciating that she had to be hospitalized and given morphine to endure it.

Her story and her desire to find protection in the promises of Scripture reminded me of my own experience of wondering how to apply some of the passages in the Bible that seemed like promises I could claim—certainly promises I wanted to claim.

About nine months after Hope died, the assignment in the Bible study group I was a part of was to read Psalm 91 and express how it had been true in my life.

He will rescue you from every trap
and protect you from deadly disease.
He will cover you with his feathers.
He will shelter you with his wings.

His faithful promises are your armor and
    protection. . . .
If you make the LORD your refuge,
    if you make the Most High your shelter,
no evil will conquer you;
    no plague will come near your home.
For he will order his angels
    to protect you wherever you go.
They will hold you up with their hands
    so you won't even hurt your foot on a stone. . . .
The LORD says, "I will rescue those who love me.
    I will protect those who trust in my name."

PSALM 91:3-4, 9-12, 14

These are the kinds of verses we write out on a card to someone or turn into a screen saver. The words weave together a blanket of protection we want to wrap around ourselves to protect us from harm. But that day as I read them, they seemed like empty promises.

So as my discussion group came to this question, I had to say what I really thought. Through tears I told the group, "I don't get how this is true. He did *not* protect my family from a deadly disease. He did *not* keep us from hurting our feet on a stone but, in fact, allowed much worse than that."

At that low point in my grief, I simply wasn't willing to gloss over these verses that seemed so far removed from my reality. I didn't know how to reconcile this passage with my experience.

But I wanted to.

My solid confidence in the integrity of God's Word told me that there must be something foundational that I did not understand for it to appear to me that this passage was not true. I wanted to figure out how the scriptural promises of protection apply—not only to me, but also to the missionary who is raped, the Chinese pastor who is imprisoned, the godly mother of three who succumbs to cancer. I figured that if I could come to an understanding of what God's promises of protection mean, then there would be a breakthrough for me in my understanding of God and in my experience of loss.

So I began to work my way through the Old and New Testaments, trying to figure out what God really means when he promises to protect us, and what he has promised to protect us from. When I came to the Gospels, I could hear Jesus speaking to the issue, but it wasn't necessarily what I wanted to hear.

Jesus Prepares Us for the Worst

In Matthew 10, we come to the scene in which Jesus had just called his twelve disciples and was preparing to send them out in twos for ministry. In preparing them, he bestowed on them his own supernatural power to show his sovereignty over all physical and spiritual realms.

Jesus called his twelve disciples together and gave
them authority to cast out evil spirits and to heal
every kind of disease and illness.

MATTHEW 10:1

Jesus had much to tell the twelve before they headed out in different directions. Far from giving a pump-you-up pep talk to reassure them, he seemed to be preparing them for the worst. "You will be handed over to the courts and will be flogged with whips in the synagogues," he told them (verse 17). "When you are arrested, don't worry about how to respond or what to say," he instructed (verse 19). "All nations will hate you because you are my followers," he predicted (verse 22).

And then he said something that especially catches my attention.

Don't be afraid of those who want to kill you. They
can only kill your body; they cannot touch your soul.
Fear only God, who can destroy both soul and body
in hell.

MATTHEW 10:28

I can't help but want to say in response, "They can *only* kill my body? And this should be a relief to me?"

Jesus' words reveal that there is something far more important to him than protecting us from physical harm. His agenda is Kingdom advancement. His cause may cost us our lives, and evidently he is okay with that.

When I say he is okay with that, I don't mean he is passive about it or applauds it. He cares deeply about what happens to us, and we need to hear him say that, too, in the very next verse:

> *What is the price of two sparrows—one copper coin?*
> *But not a single sparrow can fall to the ground*
> *without your Father knowing it. And the very hairs*
> *on your head are all numbered. So don't be afraid;*
> *you are more valuable to God than a whole flock*
> *of sparrows.*
>
> MATTHEW 10:29-31

Do you hear Jesus speaking to you in this, making sure you hear how valuable you are to him, how carefully and lovingly he knows you? We can never think he is uncaring about the difficulties we face as we live in this world for him.

But when we look at Jesus' life and violent death, when we consider the lives and deaths of his disciples, and when we listen to what Jesus said over and over again about how we will receive rewards for enduring persecution for his sake, it becomes obvious that there is something more important to Jesus than our bodily comfort and safety. While he cares deeply about us and the physical pain we experience, he cares far more about our spiritual conditions. He knows that these bodies of ours are wearing out and will die before the day comes when he raises them up and renews them. It's our souls that he is most concerned about.

Jesus knows we have a hard time grasping this more significant spiritual reality. Limited by these bodies and our earthly perspectives, it is hard for us to imagine our eternal future and how the way we live now and what we believe now will impact that eternal reality. And so in our everyday requests for safe travel and physical health, and in our more desperate prayers for healing or deliverance amid great difficulties, we try to apply to our bodies God's promises of protection that were intended for our souls. And when we do, we're often left disappointed.

There is something more important to Jesus than our bodily comfort and safety.

When God doesn't seem to show up and protect us, we can quickly point the finger of blame, accusing him of falling down on the job. Until our value systems line up with his, until we value the eternal life of our souls more than the temporary life of our earthly bodies, we will continue to feel disappointed with God.

God has not promised wholesale physical deliverance in this life for those who place their faith in him. But he has promised to protect our souls for eternity. And really that is so much bigger, so much better.

It doesn't necessarily seem more significant to you and me here and now . . . but it is.

Overhearing Jesus Pray for Us

"I'm praying for you." Those words mean a lot when we're hurting. Someone cares enough to lift our names and our needs before the Father. And we know their prayers make a difference. "The earnest prayer of a righteous person has great power and produces wonderful results" (James 5:16). We don't always know what those results will be, but we can be sure that prayer matters and prayer produces.

I suppose this amazes me because we don't really know how to pray, do we? We long to be earnest in prayer, but so often we dabble at prayer. If we're honest, sometimes our prayers are intended more for the ears of the people listening to us than for the Father's ears. Our prayers tend to be inconsistent, self-centered, and energized more by a desire to get what we want from God than to enter into what he wants.

But there is one who prays for us whose prayers are never insincere or misguided. His prayers are earnest to the core. He is the only truly righteous person who has ever lived. So certainly the earnest prayers of this righteous person have great power and produce wonderful results.

Of course I'm talking about Jesus. In John 17, John records Jesus' prayer for his disciples. Jesus made it clear, however, that his prayer was not only for his close inner circle of apostles. "I am praying not only for these disciples but also for all who will ever believe in me through their message," Jesus said (verse 20). If you believe in Jesus, then Jesus prayed this prayer for you:

> *Holy Father, you have given me your name; now*
> *protect them by the power of your name. . . . I'm not*
> *asking you to take them out of the world, but to keep*
> *them safe from the evil one.*
>
> JOHN 17:11, 15

When we read Jesus' prayer in John 17, a prayer of protection and safety for his disciples that is extended to all who will ever believe, we can't help but feel privileged and hopeful for the future. Surely God answers the prayers of Jesus with a resounding *yes!*

We might expect that God's affirmative answer to Jesus' prayer would mean that the disciples would never face any harm, right? But we know that isn't what happened. History records that all but one of the disciples were killed for their allegiance to Christ. Only John is said to have lived to old age, and he was severely persecuted for the sake of the gospel. Most of the disciples spent years in prison and were stoned, beheaded, or crucified.

So how do we reconcile Jesus' prayer of protection for the disciples with the reality that nearly every one of them died a martyr's death? Is that how God protects those he loves?

Jesus asked his Father to protect the disciples and us from

the evil one, because he knows that the devil wants to destroy us. In fact, according to 1 Peter 5:8, Satan "prowls around like a roaring lion, looking for someone to devour." And how does he devour us? Satan brings suffering in an effort to diminish our faith, he brings temptation in an attempt to deceive us, and he brings doubt about God's love and goodness to try to estrange us from God. Satan's goal in this world is to keep us alienated from God and claim us as his own for eternity.

How do we reconcile Jesus' prayer of protection for the disciples with the reality that nearly every one of them died a martyr's death? Is that how God protects those he loves?

But Jesus has prayed for us, asking his Father to protect us from the evil one, so we are not at Satan's mercy. God has answered the prayer of Jesus with a resounding *yes!* and all those who are in Christ are safe from the damning power of the evil one. While Satan may win a battle or two in the life of the believer, he will never win the war against the soul. Jesus has prayed for his own, and we are protected.

Jesus Promises to Provide Protection

Certainly one of the most politically incorrect words in the English language today is *judgment*. And the idea that God will judge sin is considered an old-fashioned, out-of-date scare tactic. But Scripture is clear that judgment for sin is certain and will be terrifying for those who are not protected from it.

Jesus spoke often of the judgment and wrath that are coming against sin. "Anyone who believes in God's Son has eternal life," Jesus said. But he went on to say, "Anyone who doesn't obey the Son will never experience eternal life but remains under God's angry judgment" (John 3:36).

Paul writes,

> *A day of anger is coming, when God's righteous judgment will be revealed. He will judge everyone according to what they have done. . . . He will pour out his anger and wrath on those who live for themselves, who refuse to obey the truth and instead live lives of wickedness.*
>
> ROMANS 2:5-6, 8

One day the wrath of God against sin is going to be poured out.

Now, we would much rather talk about God's love than God's wrath, but isn't it a relief to know that evil in this world will not go unpunished, that justice will be done? Well, it's a relief to me . . . until I look into my own heart and recognize that the evil within me deserves nothing less than the wrath of God.

So if the wrath of God against sin is certain and the evil inside me is unavoidable, then is my experience of that wrath inevitable? Is there anything or anyone who can protect me from the wrath of God that is going to fall, flowing out of his divine justice?

Hear Jesus speaking into this sorrowful situation. He says that this is exactly why he came, that he will protect those who come to him. He will keep us safe.

> *God sent his Son into the world not to judge the world, but to save the world through him.*
>
> JOHN 3:17

As we hide ourselves in the person and work of Jesus, we find shelter and safety from the sure and certain wrath of God.

Jesus is able to protect us from the wrath of God only because there was no protection for him. As he hung on the cross, he absorbed the wrath of God in our place so that we could be protected from it. Paul writes, "Since we have been made right in God's sight by the blood of Christ, he will certainly save us from God's condemnation" (Romans 5:9).

Jesus is able to protect us from the wrath of God only because there was no protection for him.

When I open my eyes to see Jesus on the cross, I can no longer harbor resentment that he hasn't come through for me in the ways I have wanted him to—ways that are so limited by my earthly perspective. I can no longer insist that his promises of protection apply to everything that threatens my comfortable existence in this life. I realize he has paid the ultimate price so that I can be protected from the wrath I deserve. And I hear Jesus speaking into my sorrow, saying that *this* is how he protects those he loves.

Jesus speaks into our craving for safety and security, helping us to see that he is protecting us in ways that are vaster than we could ever define or demand. His promises of protection go much deeper than protecting our bodies or our agendas or our plans for our lives.

Jesus has prayed for our protection. He has provided our protection. We can rest easy, knowing we're protected. We're safe.

As He Protects You in the Storm

⚜

I HEAR THE LONGING in your heart for security and safety—especially as you live in a world that is being shaken by so much difficulty and heartache. Don't be surprised by the hardship, and don't let your heart be troubled by it. Trust in God, and trust in me. You can find real peace and lasting security only as you find your home in me.

I can give you a solid foundation to build on so you can withstand the storms of life. Come to me, and really listen to what I am saying to you in my Word. Read it, think it through, dig deeply into it, and then work it into your life. Let it shape your thoughts and your values, your priorities and your day-to-day conduct. If you do, you'll find that while storms still blow into your life, you won't be destroyed by them. Your world may be rocked by difficulty and disappointment, but your faith will hold firm.

Find comfort in the truth that I am preparing a place where you will be safe and secure forever with me. There will be no storms, no threats, and no fear—only perfect peace and safety. This sure hope is a strong and trustworthy anchor for your soul when the winds of difficulty are blowing in your life. It is a promise you can depend on. Take hold of it and live like you believe it.

Adapted from John 14:1; 16:33; Luke 6:46-49; John 14:2; 2 Timothy 4:18; Hebrews 6:18-19

Chapter 6

HEAR JESUS SAYING,
I Have a Purpose in Your Pain

"This happened so the power of God could be seen in him." JOHN 9:3

Jesus gives us insight when we ask, "Why?"

As I awoke in the hospital the morning after we received Hope's dismal diagnosis, reality came rushing back to my consciousness. One of my first thoughts was, *This is my fault. I didn't pray enough for a healthy baby. If only I had prayed more faithfully, God wouldn't have needed to do this to get my attention.* Like many people who experience difficulty, I immediately made the assumption that my suffering was my fault, that all my sins had caught up with me and I was finally getting what I deserved.

Why? is the question that seems to haunt most people who suffer deeply. In fact, many of us get stuck there. Until we get an acceptable answer to this question, we can't move forward.

In asking why, I think we really have two questions. We want to know what caused the suffering, as well as what purpose there is in it. We want to know what or who is responsible and then figure out if there was any good reason for it.

Jesus spoke to both those questions in his response to his disciples, who asked him why a man begging outside the Temple had been born blind. But they didn't really ask *why* that directly. They made an assumption—an assumption that was common in their day. According to rabbinical teaching, all suffering was directly attributed to acts of sin, either by the affected person or by his or her parents. Some rabbis taught that children could sin in the womb and then pay the penalty all their lives for prenatal sin. So the disciples assumed that someone's specific sin was directly responsible for the man's blindness—they just didn't know whose.

> *"Rabbi," his disciples asked him, "why was this man born blind? Was it because of his own sins or his parents' sins?"*
> JOHN 9:2

In many ways their assumptions echo those of the friends of Job, one of the Old Testament's most significant sufferers. Job was considered "blameless—a man of complete integrity" (Job 1:1), yet he experienced the loss of his property, his ten children, and his health. Job's friends were convinced that he must have committed a secret sin for him to have to endure such devastating losses. The basic assumption of Job's friends was that his suffering was his fault—that God rained down suffering on his life to make him pay for some grievous wrong.

And there is a part of us that thinks that way too, isn't there? Who of us has not experienced something that has caused us to think, *Finally my mistake has caught up with me—now I'm going to pay*?

There is something deep inside us that tells us that we get what we deserve, or maybe that we deserve what we get. But is that really how it works? Does God make us pay for our disobedience with suffering?

Our instincts might tell us it should work that way. But our instincts are often unreliable. The truth is, if you belong to Jesus, you never have to agonize over the assumption that your suffering is God's way of making you pay for the mistakes you've made. You can be confident that your suffering is not a punishment for your sin. And how do I know that?

> *He was punished for your sin so you don't have to be.*

Because someone has already been punished for your sin.

All the punishment for your bad choices—your outright rebellion, your utter apathy toward God, your ugliest, most shameful actions—has all been laid on Jesus. He was punished for your sin so you don't have to be.

That is the gospel. And it goes against our instincts. It seems too good to be true. Jesus has endured the punishment we deserve and offered to us his own perfect record of righteousness. When we hide ourselves in the person of Jesus, we don't have to fear that God is going to take out his anger on us for the wrong we've done. He poured out that anger on Jesus at the Cross so that he can pour out his forgiveness on us.

So if our suffering in this life isn't a punishment for our sin, what is it? What causes it? Why does it happen?

The Cause of Our Suffering

While our suffering is never punishment for our sin, certainly we experience the natural consequences of our sin. Proverbs 22:8 says, "Those who plant injustice will harvest disaster." We all recognize that we bring a lot of our suffering on ourselves through our own bad choices. God does not step in to shield us from suffering the natural consequences imposed on us from living as imperfect humans in this world. And it's not just the natural consequences of our own sins that cause us suffering. We often suffer the natural consequences of the sins of people around us too.

Other times our suffering is just the natural result of living in a fallen, broken world, where accidents happen and natural disasters strike and bodies age. So much of our pain is the natural result of living in a world that is broken to the core because of the effects of sin.

There was a time when life here wasn't like that—when pain

was not a part of human experience. But everything changed when we as humans chose to look for satisfaction apart from God. The book of Romans helps us understand: "When Adam sinned, sin entered the world. Adam's sin brought death, so death spread to everyone, for everyone sinned" (Romans 5:12). This death curse cut deeper than just humanity. It impacted all of creation: "Against its will, all creation was subjected to God's curse" (Romans 8:20).

Our world is broken because of the devastating effects of sin, and we regularly experience that brokenness in the form of suffering. Death, disease, destruction—these are all the result of living in a world where sin has taken root and corrupted everything.

When something bad happens, we can be so quick to get mad at God, laying the blame for our suffering at his doorstep. But I sometimes wonder why nobody ever exclaims when they suffer, "I am so mad at sin!" Shouldn't we lay the blame for suffering where it belongs? Shouldn't the suffering of this world make us really mad at sin and the power it has to hurt us and those we love? Shouldn't it cause us to be grateful that God hates sin and the suffering it causes so much that he was willing to send his Son to die to free this world from the curse and brokenness of sin?

The process for ridding our world of its brokenness began when Jesus became flesh and took the curse upon himself. He set in motion a process of relief from this curse and restoration to perfection, but that process is not yet complete. For now, we are living in an in-between time until that day comes, so suffering is a bitter reality of the world we live in. As a result, we should expect natural disasters, deadly viruses, and defective genes—because this world is broken, and it will continue to be broken until Christ ushers in a new heaven and a new earth in which there is no more curse.

I sometimes wonder why nobody ever exclaims when they suffer, "I am so mad at sin!"

In addition to natural consequences and natural causes, surely some suffering is the supernatural work of Satan. Satan's goal is to alienate us from God. This is evidenced most clearly in the story of Job, in which Satan came to God and asked permission to harm Job in an attempt to prove that Job was faithful to God only because of the blessings God gave him. If the blessings went away, Satan was convinced Job would turn his back against God, and he set out to prove it (Job 1:9-11). Likewise, Jesus talked about Satan's supernatural involvement in suffering when he said to Simon Peter, "Simon, Simon, Satan has asked to sift each of you like wheat. But I have pleaded in prayer for you, Simon, that your faith should not fail" (Luke 22:31-32). It is interesting to note that Satan's purpose in both Job's and Peter's situation is the same, and it tells us something about why Satan brings suffering into our lives. He wants to drive a wedge between us and God. He uses suffering as a tool to seek to destroy our faith and confidence in God.

Interestingly, the same tool of suffering that Satan seeks to use to *destroy* our faith is, in the hands of God, a tool God plans to use to *develop* our faith. The same circumstance that Satan sends to tempt us to reject God is what God uses to train us. What Satan inflicts to wound us, God intends to prune us.

The writer of Hebrews tells us that "the LORD disciplines those he loves" and that "no discipline is enjoyable while it is happening—it's painful!" (Hebrews 12:6, 11). This shows us that some of the suffering we experience is actually the loving discipline of our Father. "Endure this divine discipline," the writer encourages. "God's discipline is always good for us" (Hebrews 12:7, 10). Obviously discipline doesn't feel good at the time. It feels like hardship and loss, and it often brings sorrow. What allows us as God's children to endure it is that while it's painful, we're confident it's purposeful. Never punitive. Never random. Never too harsh. Always out of love. What's the purpose? God's desire is that "afterward there will be a peaceful harvest of right living for those who are trained in this way" (Hebrews 12:11). God is at work cutting away the dead places and destructive patterns in our lives so we can flourish and grow.

So in looking for what or who has brought suffering into our lives, we can't ignore the reality that because God is ultimately in control of this world and our lives, nothing happens to us that has not been appointed by him. I recognize that this idea makes many people uncomfortable, and most of us would rather say that while God may "allow" suffering into our lives, he would never initiate it, send it, or be in any way behind it. That just doesn't seem right.

Certainly it is true that God allows suffering. We see that over and over in Scripture. But we also see that he often appears to be more active than simply allowing us to experience the natural consequences of sin, the inevitable results of the brokenness of this world, or the fiery darts of Satan.

So while it is not inaccurate to say that God *allows* evil and suffering, it is inadequate, and perhaps misleading, to limit God's involvement in suffering to this word, suggesting that he only passively (and perhaps reluctantly, we hope) gives permission. In fact, there are only a handful of scriptural passages where the text itself says that God "allowed" or "permitted" difficulty or harm, while many more indicate that God sent, intended, brought about, planned, caused, or gave experiences of suffering to his people for some purpose (Deuteronomy 32:39; 2 Samuel 12:15; Psalm 66:10-12; Isaiah 45:7; Jeremiah 46:28; Jonah 2:3; Matthew 4:1; 1 Peter 3:17).

Over the centuries, far greater minds than mine have considered and debated the role of God in suffering, and there is still much disagreement on how best to articulate this holy mystery. I fully recognize and respect that many faithful believers will say only that God "allows" suffering into our lives. Perhaps part of our struggle is the inadequacy of our language—we are limited by mere words in our discussion of God's role in suffering, which is beyond our complete comprehension and articulation.

But as we take Scripture at face value, we see that God did not merely allow many of the events and actions we would label as bad or evil, but he actively sent them, intended them, gave them. Perhaps the best word is that he *ordained* them, meaning he is the first cause behind everything. By his overriding, providential control, all his purposes are accomplished in our world and in our lives. While God never does evil, he does ordain it to come about through secondary causes, and yet in the process he does not become blameworthy. Several examples from Scripture may help to clarify:

Joseph's suffering. Joseph was betrayed by his brothers, imprisoned by Potiphar, and forgotten by the cupbearer (Genesis 37; 39–40). They are each responsible for the evil done to Joseph. Yet Joseph clearly saw God behind the suffering inflicted by his brothers when he said to them, "It was God who sent me here, not you! And he is the one who made me an adviser to Pharaoh" (Genesis 45:8), and later, "You intended to harm me, but *God intended* it all for good. He brought me to this position so I could save the lives of many people" (Genesis 50:20, emphasis added). This speaks to God's active intentions and not merely a decision, after the fact, to turn to good or use for good what he allowed. The psalmist reflected on God's ordaining this series of events, saying, "[The Lord] called for a famine on the land of Canaan, cutting off its food supply. Then he sent someone to Egypt ahead of them—Joseph, who was sold as a slave" (Psalm 105:16-17).

Job's suffering. Satan asked God's permission to inflict Job with suffering, and God certainly allowed it. The text makes it plain that "*Satan . . .* struck Job with terrible boils" (Job 2:7, emphasis added). But Job then said, "The LORD gave me what I had, and the LORD has taken it away" (1:21). Later he asked his wife the question, "Should we accept only good things from the hand of God and never anything bad?" (2:10). So Job obviously saw his suffering as ultimately coming from God, and God described it that way too, saying to Satan, "You urged me to harm him without cause" (2:3). Then in the last chapter of Job, the inspired author writes, "They consoled him and comforted him because of all the trials *the LORD* had brought against him" (42:11, emphasis added). It doesn't indicate that God merely allowed the trouble but that he "brought [it] against him."

The children of Israel's suffering. Throughout the Old Testament, the children of Israel are taken into captivity, are defeated in battle, and suffer in many other ways. Certainly their captors and other enemies are responsible for the evil and cruelty inflicted upon them. And yet Scripture repeatedly describes these experiences as God's preordained plan, something he orchestrated to happen, not only to put his glorious nature on display, but also to accomplish his good purpose in the lives of his people—to refine them and cause them to call out to him and to return to him. Just a few examples: Genesis 15:13-14, in which God says, "You can be sure that your descendants will be strangers in a foreign land, where they will be oppressed as slaves for 400 years. But I will punish the nation that enslaves them, and in the end they will come away with great wealth." Deuteronomy 4:27-29 says, "The LORD will scatter you among the nations, where only a few of you will survive. There, in a foreign land, you will worship idols. . . . But from there you will search again for the LORD your God." Numbers 21:6-7 says that "the LORD sent poisonous snakes among the people, and many were bitten and died. Then the people came to Moses and cried out, 'We have sinned.'" Psalm 78:32-39 includes, "When God began killing them, they finally sought him." In Jeremiah 15:14, 19 God says, "I will tell your enemies to take you as captives to a foreign land. . . . If you return to me, I will restore you so you can continue to serve me." And in Amos 3:6 the prophet asks the rhetorical question, "Does disaster come to a city unless the LORD has planned it?"

Jesus' suffering. To me the most compelling argument against limiting our verbiage and understanding to God's merely allowing suffering is what Jesus endured on the cross. Certainly we would not suggest that God simply allowed Jesus to be crucified in the same way we would suggest that God only allows the losses in our lives. In fact, we know the Cross was God's preordained plan (John 12:27; Acts 2:23;

4:27-28; 1 Corinthians 2:7-8) that he brought to fulfillment. Isaiah writes about it in Isaiah 53, speaking prophetically of Jesus, "it was the LORD's good plan to crush him and cause him grief" (verse 10).

It seems intellectually dishonest and scripturally uninformed for me to thank God and give him credit for doing the things in my life that I would label "good" and "beneficial" but then to suggest he has been passive in the things I might label "bad" or "harmful." Instead I must recognize his supreme sovereignty over all of my life—that nothing happens to me outside of his preordained plan. And when I say that he is redeeming the hard and hurtful things in my life (and I do!), I'm not saying he is running along behind Satan, other people, or the brokenness of this world to clean up behind them, seeking to creatively turn the suffering into good after the fact. He intended it for my good all along—he is the first cause behind every other secondary cause.

On the surface this is a truth that is hard to understand and perhaps even harder to accept. And yet the alternative is far more troubling. Charles Spurgeon said it this way:

> It would be a very sharp and trying experience to me to think that I have an affliction which God never sent me, that the bitter cup was never filled by his hand, that my trials were never measured out by him nor sent to me by his arrangement of their weight and quantity. . . .

He who made no mistakes in balancing the clouds and meting out the heavens, commits no errors in measuring out the ingredients which compose the medicine of souls.

When we attempt to spare God's reputation and be at peace with his plans by insisting that he allows but never sends the hard and painful things in our lives, we diminish God's sovereignty and ultimately diminish the source and security of our hope.

When David and I ponder the question of why we've had two children who were born with a fatal syndrome, we believe we've experienced the natural result of living in a fallen, broken world in which our bodies—our very genetic codes—have been corrupted. And at the same time, we can see how God has used this to teach us and train us. And we don't believe he has done that as an afterthought. He's not making the best of a bad situation that was out of his control, but in fact, every day of Hope and Gabriel's lives, and every day of our lives, has been ordained by God from before the foundation of the world (Psalm 139:16).

God doesn't sit back as a passive observer and allow circumstances or Satan to hurt us, only to step in afterward and say optimistically, "I can make this into something good!" He has a purpose and design in what is happening to us from the beginning, and even though what is happening to us might not *be* good, God intends it all for our ultimate good.

What matters in the end is not that we know what or whom to assign responsibility to. What matters is that we are convinced that God loves us and that his love is not merely sentimental or a commitment to our comfort. We know his love is an active commitment to our ultimate good and our eternal happiness.

When the winds of sorrow and doubt and questions and pain were blowing the hardest in my life, there were a couple of solid things I grabbed hold of that kept me from being swept away into alienation from God. Certainly the most significant truth I held on to was a solid belief that Romans 8:28 is really true—that God can and will use everything, no matter how dark, for my ultimate good, because I am his. That doesn't mean I'm a Pollyanna about the sufferings of life or that I diminish the evil or pain associated with the hurts of this life. I'm saying that when we grab hold of the confidence that God is using the worst things we can imagine for our ultimate good, we can see the light beyond the darkness. The second thing I've held on to is my firm belief that God loves me. It is his love that enables me to accept his sovereignty.

His love is an active commitment to our ultimate good and our eternal happiness.

And when I've found his love and sovereignty in hardship difficult to believe, difficult to swallow, what has helped me most is to look at the Cross. Because when we look at the Cross, we see the most innocent victim, the most immense suffering, the greatest injustice, the most hurtful betrayal, the greatest physical and emotional agony. Surely the Cross was the greatest evil of all time.

But it was also the most precious gift God has ever given, the greatest good ever accomplished. Because of the Cross, we don't get what we deserve—punishment for our sin. Instead, we get what we don't deserve—the mercy and forgiveness of God. When we look at the Cross, it fills us with confidence that God is sovereign over everything—including evil. And if he can use something as evil as the Cross of Christ for such amazing good, I can believe he can use what I would label as evil in my life for good.

> *If he can use something as evil as the Cross of Christ for such amazing good, I can believe he can use what I would label as evil in my life for good.*

The Purpose in Our Suffering

Jesus answered the disciples' question about why the man was born blind by saying, "It was not because of his sins or his parents' sins. . . . This happened so the power of God could be seen in him" (John 9:3). In a sense, Jesus seemed to ignore their question about why it happened in terms of what caused it. It was as if Jesus wanted to move them from seeking the *cause* to seeking the *purpose.* And he stated it clearly: "*so that* the work of God might be displayed in his life" (NIV, emphasis added).

And this is where we need to lean in to listen to hear Jesus speaking to us in our sorrow. Because he wants to do the same thing with us. He wants us to stop being stuck on figuring out the cause of our suffering so we can fulfill the purpose he has in our suffering. His purpose for your suffering and my suffering is the same as it was for this man's suffering—that in the midst of it, we would put the work of God in our lives on display for the world to see.

But wait a minute, we want to say. *God put his power on display in that man's life by giving him sight—by doing a miracle.*

The work of God seems obvious in this story and in so many others in the Gospels that describe the way God miraculously healed people and even resurrected people from the dead. And it seems obvious in the lives of those around us whose relationships are restored and whose endeavors see success and whose bodies are healed. It is less obvious in the lives of those of us who don't get the miracle.

Or is it?

Somewhere along the way with Hope, I remember someone saying to David and me, "The miracle likely isn't going to be that God will heal Hope. The miracle is going to be that God will heal you."

Whoever you were who said that to us—you were right. The Spirit of God working in us to give us a spirit of acceptance and even joy in the midst of tremendous sorrow has produced nothing less than a miracle. Hope and peace beyond our human capacity to generate and maintain have shown us that God is at work in us and through us in a way we can't explain or take credit for.

We have gotten a taste of what Paul describes in 2 Corinthians 4:

> *We are pressed on every side by troubles, but we*
> *are not crushed. We are perplexed, but not driven*
> *to despair. We are hunted down, but never aban-*
> *doned by God. We get knocked down, but we are not*
> *destroyed. . . . That is why we never give up. Though*
> *our bodies are dying, our spirits are being renewed*
> *every day.*
>
> 2 CORINTHIANS 4:8-9, 16

To experience and exude peace when life is crashing down around you, to have the lightness of joy when the weight of sorrow is heavy, to be grateful for what God has given you when you've lost what is most precious to you—that is God at work on the interior of your life, on display in your life. It is the light of God piercing the darkness of this world.

Certainly all this is part of God's purpose for the suffering and sorrow in your life.

Can you hear Jesus speaking into your sorrow, telling you that he has a purpose for your pain, a good purpose that will infuse your loss with meaning as you show the world the difference a connectedness to Jesus makes in the lowest places of life?

Honestly, I've come to think that looking for a specific answer to the question *Why?* is mostly an unsatisfying quest. What we really are in search of is not an explanation but a sense of meaning. We want to know that there is some meaning and purpose in our losses—that they are not random or worthless. We want to see the ways God is using our loss for good.

Sometimes God, in his goodness, draws back the curtain and shows us; we can see how he is using our loss in our lives or in the lives of those around us. And other times we have to wait. Certainly we can never expect to see the complete purposes of God in this life.

That is where faith is required—faith that God is working out all things for the good of those who love him, faith that the day will come when what we can't see now will become clear, faith that he will give us the grace we need to put his glory on display for the world to see.

As He Gives You More of Himself

————— 🌿 —————

WHEN YOU ASK ME to bless your plans and projects, I wonder if you really know what you are asking for. To be blessed is to experience and know more of me. To ask me to bless your life and your efforts is to invite me into the center of it. That is the essence of blessing, the joy of it. Oh, how I long to bless you! I want to share from my abundance one gracious blessing after another.

To be blessed is to be deeply secure and content in me. It is to make your home so securely in me that nothing can shake you. You can be blessed in the midst of a miserable situation, because being blessed doesn't mean you have no trouble or struggle or sorrow; it doesn't mean you always experience success and comfort. It means that in the midst of the trouble and struggle and sorrow, you find yourself deeply secure, profoundly content and happy in me.

To know me and walk with me and share life with me is the essence of blessing. And the truth is, it is the hard things in your life that cause you to want to know me more intimately, walk with me more closely, and share life with me more fully. That is why, in the losses of life, you can find yourself blessed beyond your imagination or expectation. Because you have found more of me in these hard places. You've moved from just hearing my Word to living it—putting it to the test. You're finding that giving is better than receiving, neediness is better than self-sufficiency, trust is better than worry. You've discovered that my Word is true, my joy is your strength, my promises are your hope, my presence is your comfort.

Others may look at the sorrow of your situation and express regret. But when you get to the bottom of your grief and find more of me than you've experienced and known before, you can look other people in the eye and say, "Please don't feel sorry for me. I am incredibly blessed," and really mean it.

Adapted from John 1:16; Matthew 16:17; Luke 11:28; Luke 1:45; John 20:29; Matthew 5–7; Acts 20:35; Philippians 4:11-13

Chapter 7

HEAR JESUS SAYING,

I Will Give You a Heart for Forgiveness

"When you are praying, first forgive anyone you are holding a grudge against, so that your Father in heaven will forgive your sins, too." MARK 11:25

Jesus empowers us to forgive people who don't deserve it.

I don't know about you, but the topic of forgiveness makes me a little uncomfortable. It's an area of ongoing struggle in my life. I know what it is to be so deeply resentful that the very suggestion I should forgive is repugnant. I know what it is to want to hold on to my justified anger and presumed moral superiority. I often find myself rehearsing conversations with those who have offended me in which I cunningly lay out for them the utter corruption of what they've said or done. In my own mind, I lay them low with my words. Because I want them to hurt like they hurt me. Somehow I've fooled myself into thinking that will bring me pleasure. And more than that, I've convinced myself it would be good and right to set them straight.

Then I read, "When you are praying, first forgive anyone you are holding a grudge against, so that your Father in heaven will forgive your sins, too" (Mark 11:25). When I hear Jesus telling me to forgive anyone I have developed a grudge against before I seek to make myself at home in his presence, I don't particularly relish the thought of what that will mean for me. And when I hear Jesus say I can't expect to have my sins forgiven by God if I stubbornly refuse to extend forgiveness to others, I feel backed into an uncomfortable corner.

So what are we to do with Jesus' repeated instructions to forgive that are woven throughout the Gospels? How can we ever hope to overcome our internal resistance to letting go of the resentment that has made itself so at home in our hearts?

To forgive will cost us something. And I think Jesus might say, "Yes it will. But it will be worth it. I know. I have paid the price for forgiveness with my own lifeblood."

To forgive will take a miracle. And perhaps Jesus would say, "Yes it will. So you will need me like never before. And I am here, offering my Spirit to accomplish nothing less than something supernatural."

What about Your Justifiable Resentment?

So much of what Jesus says about forgiveness in the Gospels refers to those who have sinned against us. For example, at one point Peter came to Jesus with this question:

*"Lord, how often should I forgive someone who sins
against me? Seven times?"*
*"No, not seven times," Jesus replied, "but seventy
times seven!"*

MATTHEW 18:21-22

I get caught there because I realize it would be hard to categorize much of what I've been slow to forgive in others as sin against me. Slights? Yes. Insensitivity? Yes. Selfishness? Certainly, from my standpoint. But sin?

If these offenses don't reach the level of sin against me, why am I so hurt by them?

Perhaps at other times in my life I wouldn't have even noticed the offense. I would have brushed it off, overlooked it, ignored it, maybe even laughed it off. But not when I'm laid low by sorrow.

We all know what it's like to have a burn or a physical injury and discover for the first time how much we use that part of our body. The affected area might have been bumped or brushed up against countless times before it became inflamed, but we never really noticed. Now we're much more sensitive. We notice every time someone carelessly makes contact with us. We have a heightened sensitivity, and it doesn't take much to hurt us.

That's how it is when our hearts have been broken, when our insides have been rubbed raw by difficulty or disappointment or the death of someone we love. We're far more sensitive to the thoughtless comments and dismissive slights of others. We expect more from everyone around us, and we're easily annoyed and offended when we don't get it.

And somehow in the midst of so much emotional pain, it feels good to give way to anger. It can even feel *right* to give in to anger. A sense of "this is not how it should be" rises up in us, and we set out on a mission to make things right—or to at least make sure others know what they have done wrong.

Of course, many of us have experienced far deeper hurts than simply being overlooked or offended. These deeper hurts—such as betrayal, abandonment, and abuse—make forgiveness seem an especially tall order, or pretty much impossible. When someone who should have been there for us didn't show up, when someone who should be for us has turned against us, it hurts. Deeply. Unspeakably.

> *Somehow in the midst of so much emotional pain, it feels good to give way to anger. It can even feel* right *to give in to anger.*

I recently spent some time with a woman who lost her son in an automobile accident, and while she has found so much healing from the pain of her loss, there is still a smoldering anger deep inside for the driver, who was severely intoxicated and has never made an apology. She recently came face-to-face with him in the aisle of a grocery store and had to turn her cart around and go the other way. I don't blame her, do you?

Certainly Jesus couldn't have had that kind of hurt in mind when he said, "If you hold anything against anyone, forgive him" (Mark 11:25, NIV). Didn't he know that people like that don't *deserve* to be forgiven?

Yes, he knows. Because he has forgiven people who have hardly begun to see how deeply they've offended him, people who keep committing the same offenses over and over with barely a thought, people who simply don't deserve to be forgiven. People like me. And you.

Last Sunday morning during Communion at our church, I was struck by the Scripture our pastor quoted: "Then he took the cup, gave thanks and offered it to them, saying, 'Drink from it, *all of you.* This is my blood of the covenant, which is poured out *for many* for the forgiveness of sins'" (Matthew 26:27-28, NIV, emphasis added).

I was moved by the openhanded generosity of Jesus' forgiveness. Jesus was hours away from the Cross, where the penalty of sin would come down on him and consume him. He knew what it would cost him to offer you and me forgiveness for what we've done and for who we are. And in his kindness and generosity, he was willing to absorb the hurt and offer us generous forgiveness. There was no stinginess or hesitation, no sense of coldness toward us, no determination to make us pay for what we've done. He was willing to pay the cost required for our forgiveness.

And it is only by seeing clearly both the enormity of our

offense against him and the generosity of his forgiveness toward us that we can begin to dislodge the grip that bitterness has around our hearts.

That's no doubt what Jesus had in mind when he told a parable about an unforgiving debtor in Matthew 18:21-35. There are really two debtors in the story, and the difference is in the amount they owe. The debt the servant owed the king was not just large; it was an incomprehensible amount of money, more than he could earn in a lifetime, impossible for him to repay. The debt owed to the servant by a fellow servant was about three months' wages, a pittance in comparison to the debt the servant had been forgiven.

The king's generous forgiveness toward the servant illustrates the abundance of God's forgiveness toward us. His mercy sets us free from the prison of an apparently hopeless situation, an unpayable debt. Likewise, the unwillingness of the servant to forgive the small debt of a fellow servant is an unflattering portrayal of our unrelinquished resentments and our determination to make others pay for what they've done.

When we get a true glimpse of how much God has forgiven us, when we realize that the debt we owe him is impossible to pay ourselves, we begin to find our footing for forgiving others. But until then, we may forever feel justified in refusing to forgive someone else. The debts of others that loom so large in our estimation are dwarfed when we see them in comparison to our massive offenses toward God.

Jesus' parable ends this way: "Then the angry king sent the man to prison to be tortured until he had paid his entire debt." And Jesus added, "That's what my heavenly Father will do to you if you refuse to forgive your brothers and sisters from your heart" (verses 34-35). Here we see, once again, a connection between our willingness to forgive others and God's willingness to forgive us. What exactly is the connection? Does Jesus really want to make it this black and white? Does he really mean that if we refuse to forgive others, he will not forgive us?

We simply can't say to God, "I receive your forgiveness for my sin, but I cannot forgive this fellow sinner."

Even though this parable doesn't fit comfortably into our formulas for what it means to be a part of God's family, we simply can't water it down to weaken its clear and convicting message. Jesus is saying that if we've really come into his Kingdom, we're going to be breathing in an atmosphere of generous—even sacrificial—forgiveness. Our refusal to forgive others gives evidence that we are not living and breathing in that atmosphere. It reveals that we do not value forgiveness and have not been truly and internally changed by it. Perhaps we've been exposed to it, but we haven't really experienced it firsthand.

We simply can't say to God, "I receive your forgiveness for my sin, but I cannot forgive this fellow sinner."

When Jesus teaches us to pray, he prays, "Forgive us our sins, as we have forgiven those who sin against us" (Matthew 6:12). Forgiveness flows out of a heart that has known and enjoyed forgiveness. And a person who has truly experienced the mercy of God will be merciful. Our experience of forgiveness enables us to say, "Because Jesus loves me and forgives me, I will forgive you," and really mean it.

But how, when we've been hurt so deeply?

What Does It Cost to Forgive?

What often trips us up on the pathway to forgiveness is our sense of justice. It doesn't seem at all right that the one who has hurt us can just "get away with it." How can we forgive when that person doesn't deserve it and hasn't even acknowledged what he or she did wrong? We're afraid that if we forgive, it's like saying that what that person said or did doesn't really matter—that it is excusable or not a big deal.

Jesus says that we have to become less consumed by what the person has done to hurt us or what he or she deserves and instead focus our attention on ourselves.

But forgiveness isn't minimizing what someone has done. Real forgiveness is far more costly than that. It says, "You hurt me deeply, but I'm not going to make you pay. I will pay. You don't owe me anymore— not even an apology." Forgiveness is choosing to absorb the pain and pay the debt yourself that you are rightfully owed, asking God to do a work of grace and quench the fiery anger in your heart. The process of forgiveness might lead to an honest conversation with the person who hurt you in an effort to restore the relationship and come full circle to reconciliation, but that conversation won't be a confrontation intended to get some satisfaction by making the other person feel exposed or belittled. We know we're ready for that conversation when we don't feel the sting rising up inside anymore when we think about what happened. We're ready to talk to that person when we're driven by a desire to seek reconciliation, not to deliver condemnation. In my experience, that can take some time. Sometimes a long time.

To get there, Jesus says that we have to become less consumed by what the person has done to hurt us or what he or she deserves and instead focus our attention on ourselves. In Luke 17, when Jesus speaks to the person who has been hurt by someone else, his first instructions are, "So watch yourselves!" (verse 3). Why is it that, when we are the injured party, the one in the right, we need to watch ourselves?

We need to guard our hearts against becoming fertile ground for a root of bitterness, which can go deep and wrap its tendrils around our thoughts and feelings, actions and reactions, so that we become trapped by our own resentment. We need to see ourselves clearly—our own failures, our own part in the conflict. We need to be painfully honest about the thoughtless, even cruel, things we've said and done to others. We need to watch ourselves so that we can see the logs in our own eyes (Matthew 7:3-5) before we quickly judge the faults of the people who have wronged us.

I remember coming to a humbling realization at one point on our journey with Hope. I was so sensitized to what people were saying—and not saying—to us. I knew who had reached out and who hadn't. I wondered how and why people could shrink back from expressing their concern for her and for us. Then I saw a friend whose father had recently died. And I realized I had never said anything to her about her loss. I intended to. I bought a card. But it never got sent. And after a while I just hoped that with all the people who had expressed their love and concern for her in his passing, she wouldn't notice that she had heard nothing from me.

I realized then that I had been naively unaware of the deep pain people go through during a loss, and I had rarely moved outside my comfort zone to offer words of comfort. Taking a hard look at my own failures and blindness helped me extend grace to those around me who were as oblivious as I had once been. I stopped expecting that people around me should get it and instead reminded myself, *They haven't been here. They can't know what this is like.* My heart broke as I wondered, *How many people have I hurt over the years by being unwilling to enter into their sorrow with them?*

Watching ourselves gives us perspective and keeps us humble. Watching ourselves helps to temper our anger. When we watch ourselves, we have less time and energy to make sweeping judgments about the hurtful motives and total lack of regard in the hearts of other people. It prevents us from focusing on the faults of others while forgetting our own.

As we look inside ourselves, we begin to see our own resentment as the real issue in our lives—the sin we are responsible for. We start to recognize that it's not what another person has said or done that robs us of joy but our own grudges that we've coddled and kindled. And we decide to stop throwing logs onto that fire.

As we look inside ourselves, we begin to see our own resentment as the real issue in our lives—the sin we are responsible for.

We turn off the recordings in the memories of our souls that keep replaying the painful scenes over and over, bringing a fresh sting of hurt every time. We stop allowing ourselves to entertain thoughts of how good it would feel to see those people squirm under our unanswerable arguments. We lay down our weapons of coldness and contempt. We stop constructing plans to get revenge and instead nurture thoughts of how we might bless those people. Instead of being happy when they hurt, we allow ourselves to be sad with them. We figure out what it would look like to express love in a meaningful way, and then we do it without fanfare. We refuse to keep dwelling on the injustice of what happened and choose instead to trust God to execute justice, believing that he will settle accounts for us far more justly than we can. We repent of the pride and superiority that cause us to think to ourselves, or perhaps even say out loud, *I would never do that!*

Does it seem like too tall an order? Too much of a sacrifice?

It must have seemed that way when Jesus told the disciples to forgive. Their immediate response was, "Show us how to increase our faith" (Luke 17:5). But Jesus said it wasn't more faith they needed; they already had enough. He said,

> *If you had faith even as small as a mustard seed, you could say to this mulberry tree, "May you be uprooted and thrown into the sea," and it would obey you!*
>
> LUKE 17:6

Somehow I appreciate that Jesus compares the miracle it requires for us to forgive with a mulberry tree bursting out of the soil and diving into the ocean.

Jesus was saying that if his gospel has any place at all in our hearts, we have what we need to forgive. If we have enough faith to believe that God has forgiven us our enormous debt of sin, we have what we need to forgive others.

Jesus wants to help us become as forgiving as he is.

To forgive, we need eyes of faith to see our own sin that we haven't begun to be sorry for and God's great forgiveness that we don't deserve. Just a mustard seed's worth of comprehension of the forgiveness granted to us by God is enough to break our hearts over the enormity of our own sin and the greatness of God's mercy so that we can extend mercy to someone who has hurt or offended us.

To forgive, we need resolute faith to believe that justice will be done by God and that it isn't up to us. We need humble faith to follow the example of Jesus, who "did not retaliate when he was insulted, nor threaten revenge when he suffered. He left his case in the hands of God, who always judges fairly" (1 Peter 2:23).

To forgive, we need courageous faith to move toward God by taking a step in the direction of those who have hurt us. We'd rather just shut them out and keep our distance. But instead we engage with them because we want to follow Paul's instruction to "do all that you can to live in peace with everyone" (Romans 12:18).

To forgive, we need confident faith to believe that the satisfaction of being pleasing to God will be greater than the enjoyment of putting that person in his place, forcing her to see her selfishness, ruining her reputation, making him hurt like he has hurt you.

And Jesus has given us just that kind of faith—at least a mustard seed–sized portion of it.

Jesus wants to help us become as forgiving as he is, but he knows that we don't have what it takes on our own. But then, if we are in him, we are not on our own.

As He Empowers You to Forgive

I KNOW YOU DON'T have it in your flesh to forgive, but my Holy Spirit in you can give you the power you need as you submit yourself to his work in you. I began this good work in you as I granted to you great forgiveness, and I will be faithful to complete it as it overflows in your life toward those who hurt you.

I am at work creating a soft new heart for forgiveness in place of that old hard heart of yours. As you welcome him to work, my Spirit is generating fruit in the interior of your life—loving actions in place of hateful intentions, joyful inter-actions in place of uncomfortable avoidance, peaceful thoughts in place of inner turmoil, patience in place of frustration, kind-ness in place of coldness, goodness in place of payback, gentle responses in place of harsh words, faithful endurance in place of walking away, and self-control in place of surrendering to what comes naturally.

Is this resentment really worth holding on to if it is a bar-rier between you and the one who hurt you, as well as a barrier between you and me? Won't you let it go so you can grab hold of life that is free from this heavy burden of resentment, a life so full of gratitude for being forgiven that forgiveness spills out on everyone around you?

Because you belong to me, all the self-protecting passion that keeps a flame burning under your resentment has been nailed to my cross and crucified—snuffed out. So follow the

Spirit's leading and let it go. I will be with you every step of the way, supplying the grace you need to fully forgive.

Adapted from 2 Peter 1:3; Philippians 1:6; Romans 8:13; Ezekiel 36:26; Galatians 5:16-26; Matthew 6:14-15; Colossians 3:13; 2 Corinthians 12:9

Chapter 8

HEAR JESUS SAYING,

I Am Enough for You

---

*"My grace is all you need. My power works best
in weakness."* 2 CORINTHIANS 12:9

Jesus provides what we need when we need it.

When David and I tell people about our experiences with Hope
and Gabriel, we often feel that all they can imagine is the pain
of it. We like to tell them that while it might be harder for them
to imagine, along with the pain, we experienced a great deal of
joy. During the days Hope and Gabe were with us, it wasn't all
defined by heartache.

While they were with us, there was a real richness in living.
We never knew which day might be their last, and that added
an intensity to each day.

We rarely had meaningless conversations. We talked with
everyone around us about things that really matter—like what

makes a life valuable, what it means to trust God, and what it means to love and be loved.

In the days Hope was with us, and in those first few weeks after she left us, I remember feeling full—full of insight and understanding and purpose. She had taught us so much and awakened us from the slumber of living by rote. We felt enriched by our experience with her, as she had opened up places in our hearts and in our thinking and filled them up with meaning and intentionality.

But then, as time went by, the sadness set in—a deep and pervasive sadness that went with me everywhere I went and interrupted the most mundane moments and the most intense interactions. Tears were always so close to the surface. It was as if I had a heavy weight on my chest, and I was always struggling for breath.

A few months later, though Hope had left me with such a sense of fullness, I felt completely empty—devoid of purpose, lacking energy, without insight or any sense of perspective on what had happened.

Most of us have known what it is like to be full—to be full of ideas and full of promise, to have a full plate.

Full feels good.

But now we know what it is to be empty. And empty doesn't feel so good.

One of the main ingredients of sorrow is emptiness—a deep and devastating emptiness left behind by empty promises, empty arms, an empty womb, an empty bank account, an empty place at the table, an empty bedroom, an empty bed.

But as bad as empty feels, sometimes emptiness is actually good. God can work with empty. Over and over in Scripture we see that God fills emptiness with his own power and life.

> *The earth was formless and empty, darkness was over the surface of the deep, and the Spirit of God was hovering over the waters. And God said, "Let there be light," and there was light.*
>
> GENESIS 1:2-3, NIV

> *It was by faith that even Sarah was able to have a child, though she was barren and was too old. She believed that God would keep his promise. And so a whole nation came from this one man who was as good as dead—a nation with so many people that, like the stars in the sky and the sand on the seashore, there is no way to count them.*
>
> HEBREWS 11:11-12

> *The next day there was a wedding celebration in the village of Cana in Galilee. Jesus' mother was there, and Jesus and his disciples were also invited to the celebration. The wine supply ran out during the festivities, so Jesus' mother told him, "They have no more wine."... Standing nearby were six stone water jars,*

used for Jewish ceremonial washing. Each could hold
twenty to thirty gallons. Jesus told the servants, "Fill
the jars with water." When the jars had been filled, he
said, "Now dip some out, and take it to the master of
ceremonies." So the servants followed his instructions.
. . . The master of ceremonies tasted the water that
was now wine.

JOHN 2:1-3, 6-9

Emptiness can be good when, in our emptiness, we come to
Jesus to be filled.

When we do, we have the opportunity to find out for ourselves that Jesus really can fill us up—that he can be enough
for us.

Paul's Experience of Emptiness

The apostle Paul understood emptiness. He knew what it was
to have an empty stomach, an empty wallet, and far worse.
In 2 Corinthians 11:24-27 he describes the difficulty upon
difficulty he experienced:

Five different times the Jewish leaders gave me thirty-
nine lashes. Three times I was beaten with rods.
Once I was stoned. Three times I was shipwrecked.
Once I spent a whole night and a day adrift at sea.
I have traveled on many long journeys. I have faced
danger from rivers and from robbers. I have faced

danger from my own people, the Jews, as well as from the Gentiles. I have faced danger in the cities, in the deserts, and on the seas. And I have faced danger from men who claim to be believers but are not. I have worked hard and long, enduring many sleepless nights. I have been hungry and thirsty and have often gone without food. I have shivered in the cold, without enough clothing to keep me warm.

It seems far more than any one person should have to endure, doesn't it? Did Paul ever want to say to God, "Enough already! Can't you send the shipwrecks and shackles to someone else?" We tend to think that once we've had our share, we should get a pass on any more suffering. It seems unfair to have to face trial after trial with no relief. I have to wonder if Paul ever felt that way.

Because as much as Paul had suffered, there was still more suffering in store for him. He described it in a letter to the Corinthian church: "I was given a thorn in my flesh," he wrote (2 Corinthians 12:7).

Emptiness can be good when, in our emptiness, we come to Jesus to be filled.

We don't know exactly what Paul's thorn in his flesh was, but we know it was far more than a slight discomfort. The Greek word for "thorn" is literally *stake*—a sharpened wooden shaft used to impale someone. So whatever his struggle was, Paul must have felt impaled by it, pinned down by it. Surely someone who willingly endured repeated beatings and shipwrecks and stonings and hunger and cold would not beg God again and again to remove a minor irritation. Whatever the thorn was, it brought unrelenting agony.

Why would God give Paul difficulty on top of difficulty? we want to ask. *Hadn't he endured enough?*

But interestingly, Paul didn't ask why. He knew exactly why the thorn in the flesh had been given to him. "I have received such wonderful revelations from God. *So to keep me from becoming proud*, I was given a thorn in my flesh" (2 Corinthians 12:7, emphasis added).

Paul had had an amazing experience of being caught up into the heart of ultimate spiritual reality beyond this world. The curtain of heaven was pulled back, and Paul was given a personal guided tour (2 Corinthians 12:2). It was the kind of experience that could top anyone else's claims of a special connection to God, something he could pull out to quell any questions about his authority. It was the kind of credential that could cause a person's head to swell with spiritual pride.

And evidently Paul was aware of his susceptibility to temptation in the area of pride. His awareness of this weak spot enabled him to see his painful affliction as God's provision to protect him from what would be even more painful and destructive—using his incredible spiritual experience to make himself look good.

Paul looked at the thorn and recognized in it the loving hand of God reaching into his life to prevent him from falling into the sin of boasting. And at the same time, in the same thorn, he saw the destructive hand of Satan, seeking to wreak havoc on his faith. He called the thorn in his flesh "a messenger from Satan to torment me" (2 Corinthians 12:7). Paul was tormented by the temptation to resent God for allowing the thorn to pierce his already pain-ridden life.

So often we want to nail down a singular source for our suffering. Was it God who did this to me? Did I bring this on myself? Or is there some evil force at work in my life? Paul's experience shows us that what Satan sends to destroy our faith can, at the same time, be sent by God to develop our faith. What Satan inflicts in an attempt to make us turn away from God in resentment, God intends to strengthen us as we turn toward him in dependence.

But even though Paul knew where the pain came from and why it came, ultimately it didn't matter, because he simply wanted it to go away, just like we do. We want God to reach inside our world and make the hurting stop.

Surely Paul must have thought of all the times God had shown up in supernatural ways in the past. Paul had been blinded on the road to Damascus and experienced the scales falling off his eyes so he could see again (Acts 9:1-19). He had commanded an evil spirit to come out of a slave girl (Acts 16:16-18). He had brought a man named Eutychus back to life after he fell out of a third-story window (Acts 20:9-10). Paul had laid hands on a man with fever and dysentery, and the man was healed (Acts 28:8).

But did these past miracles only add to Paul's struggle, as he wondered why God was seemingly not showing up for him now? Where was the healing touch from God for Paul, who had been the conduit of miraculous healing to so many others?

Paul asked God to take away what was causing him agonizing pain. Then he asked again. And again. And finally he heard Jesus himself speak to him. But what Jesus said was not what Paul wanted to hear. And it's not what you and I usually want to hear when we go to God with our desperate prayers.

Jesus Promises Us His Sufficiency

Jesus responded to Paul, not by giving healing, but by giving himself. Jesus said to Paul, "My grace is all you need" (2 Corinthians 12:9). Jesus spoke into Paul's emptiness and agony, saying, in essence, "I will be enough for you. I will fill up your emptiness." Jesus was telling Paul—and he's telling you and me when we repeatedly pray for relief from the pain in our lives that does not come—that he will be enough for us in whatever sorrow we are laboring under. He will strengthen us for it. We can be confident that his grace will be delivered to us in the form and quantity and timing in which we need it. He will give us the grace to endure the pain he does not take away.

When Jesus says that his grace is sufficient, he's not talking only about the grace that extends pardon for what we've done in the past. He's talking about grace that is a present power. This grace Jesus gives us is the power to go on when we think we can't make it one more day. It is the power to believe when doubts and questions are crowding into our conscious thoughts. Grace gives us what we need to take hold of God's Word and rest in it amid the voices around us and inside us that tell us God cannot be trusted.

"My power works best in weakness," Jesus says (2 Corinthians 12:9).

Jesus was telling Paul that in his weakness and brokenness, Paul would become the ideal display case for Jesus' power. When Paul was emptied of himself and his own ability to fix things, he would be prepared to experience what it means for Christ to fill him. And it's the same for us. Only when we are emptied of ourselves—our resources, our efficiency, our impressive abilities—can we experience what Paul describes: "Christ . . . fills all things everywhere with himself" (Ephesians 1:23).

We like to think that the way God can get the most glory is by doing the miracle we've put on order. We'd much rather have Jesus display his power in our lives in the form of healing and wholeness, success and accomplishment, rather than dependence and weakness. We want escape from weakness, not power in weakness. But Jesus was saying that he wanted to display his power in Paul's life not by removing the thorn but by sustaining and satisfying Paul as he lived with the thorn.

We want escape from weakness, not power in weakness.

When we are weakened by the loss in our lives and Christ's power moves in, making us content when we don't have what we need, joyful in the midst of great sadness, and at rest in the midst of chaos, God is glorified. It becomes obvious that something supernatural is happening—that the Spirit is at work on the interior of our lives, giving us the strength we need to faithfully endure whatever comes our way.

I suppose this presents a real test for us. It forces us to ask ourselves, *Do I want to experience and receive more of the grace of Jesus so I can put it on display in my life? Or do I just want him to give me what I ask for, what I think I need, so I won't have to hurt so much anymore? Can I find satisfaction when God does not fix the difficulties in my life but instead gives me the grace to endure them without complaining, without being resentful, without turning my back on him? Can I move from desperately seeking relief to diligently seeking to glorify God as I treasure him more than my own health or comfort?*

Evidently Paul passed this test. He continued to pray about the thorn in his flesh, but his prayers were no longer that the thorn would be removed. Now he prayed that this pain would be redeemed. Recognizing that the thorn would be a permanent factor in his life day to day, he prayed that he could achieve all that God wanted him to, not in spite of the thorn, but uniquely because of it.

As Paul heard Jesus speaking into his sorrow and suffering, his perspective changed completely. The pleading stopped and the power poured on. In fact, he was able to say, "That's why I *take pleasure* in my weaknesses, and in the insults, hardships, persecutions, and troubles that I suffer for Christ. For when I am weak, then I am strong" (2 Corinthians 12:10, emphasis added).

Do you think it's possible to find pleasure in the place of your deepest pain? It seems incomprehensible, even ridiculous, doesn't it?

That's because we don't really think the grace Jesus has promised us is all that good. We don't think it will be enough—not enough to fill our emptiness, not enough to meet our needs.

Can I move from desperately seeking relief to diligently seeking to glorify God as I treasure him more than my own health or comfort?

When Jesus offers himself to us in the midst of our pain, most of us think, *That's it? That's the best you can do? I was hoping for more.* The truth is, we're often more interested in getting what God's got, not getting more of God. We've put in our order for a miracle of healing or relief, and the miracle of his presence seems to us like the consolation prize.

During the season when David and I were dealing with the daily uncertainties of caring for children who were going to die, people would sometimes say to us, "I don't know how you are doing this. I could never do it."

Often we would respond by saying something that sounded a bit shocking, perhaps. "You're right. You couldn't do it. . . . God has not given you the grace for it because you don't need it, at least not right now," we would say, pausing before continuing. "But know this: when you do need it, he will give you all the grace you need."

We've put in our order for a miracle of healing or relief, and the miracle of his presence seems to us like the consolation prize.

That is what we've experienced—always enough grace for the difficulty of that day, and more grace for the next day, as we needed it. We've learned—not only because God promises it in his Word, but because we've experienced it firsthand in the lowest places of life—that the grace God has provided is all we have needed. It has been enough for whatever we have faced.

The grace God provides is enough to generate joy in the midst of your great sorrow. It's enough to enable you to endure the loneliness and the reminders of loss everywhere you turn. It's enough to keep you believing that God is good and that he loves you.

What Jesus said to Paul, he also says to you and me: "My grace is enough for you today and for everything you will face in the days to come. It will be enough—I will be enough—for whatever I allow into your life."

As He Feeds You with His Words

———————— ✦ ————————

WHEN YOU PRAY, pray like this: "Give us today the food we need for today." And then come to me asking again tomorrow. You see, I want you to learn to depend on me on a daily basis. While the world celebrates independence, I bless dependence. This is why, in the desert all those years ago, my Father sent manna to his people every morning and they could store up only enough for that day. He was teaching them daily dependence. And I want to teach you to depend on me this way too.

When my Father provided the manna to feed the bodies of God's people, he was painting a picture of how he would provide me, his Son, to feed the souls of his people. I am the true Bread from heaven that gives life to the world. Whoever comes to me will never go hungry spiritually. Whoever believes in me will find relief for their spiritual thirst.

Just as you would never expect to live very long without eating food, don't fool yourself into thinking you can live without taking in my Word. My Word is not an incidental addition to your life but your essential fuel for thriving in this world. So take into yourself the very words I have spoken. Chew on them. Let them work their way into every area of your life. Let them change you and remake you. Become saturated with my Word, and find your satisfaction in my Word.

You will never find me lacking when you come to me. As you learn to depend on me more and more, and as you discover

over and over again that I can be enough for you, you will begin to rest in my provision for you. You'll have less fear about whether or not I will show up tomorrow with what you need. You'll discover how blessed it is to hunger and thirst for me, and find me fully satisfying.

Adapted from Matthew 6:11; 2 Corinthians 1:9; Exodus 16:4; John 6:32-35; Matthew 4:4; 5:6; 6:32-33

CHAPTER 9

HEAR JESUS SAYING,

I Am Giving Life to Those Who Believe in Me

"I am the resurrection and the life. Anyone who believes in me will live, even after dying. Everyone who lives in me and believes in me will never ever die. Do you believe this?" JOHN 11:25-26

Jesus asks us to believe that death is not the end of life.

Last Easter Sunday, David and I set our alarms for 5:50 a.m.-just early enough to brush our teeth, pull on some clothes, and make it sans shower for the outdoor sunrise service at our church (okay, David took a shower, but I didn't). There weren't many of us who braved the thirty-five-degree weather, and as I looked around at the others huddled to stay warm, I realized that many of us had something in common. I saw the Moores, who buried a baby son, Sadler, so many years ago. As they carried away the Easter lily given in his memory, I knew they were thinking of him. Behind me sat Mary, whose nephew died of a brain tumor last fall, and Melanie, who buried her dad earlier this year and then her mom just a few weeks later.

And it struck me: people who have had to say good-bye to the body of someone they love are the people who recognize how much the resurrection of Jesus really matters. We want to be reminded that Jesus stands before and beyond the limits of birth and death. We've been forced into a corner, where we've come to recognize that resurrection is our only hope. And we've grabbed onto it. This promise of ongoing life has been our comfort in the face of death. Resurrection life is the basket we've put all our eggs into.

But most of us would have to admit that resurrection can seem very far away—far away in the future and far away from the reality of our deep longing to be with the people we love here and now. It can seem like a theological Band-Aid that just doesn't stop the hurt.

So we need to hear Jesus speak into our open wound. Maybe he is saying something more than we've heard so far, something that can help us heal. Maybe we need to lean in a little closer to listen to what Jesus said to some of his closest friends who were reeling in grief from the loss of their brother. "Lord," Martha said to Jesus when he arrived in Bethany four days after her brother, Lazarus, died, long after they had sent for Jesus, telling him that Lazarus was very sick, "if only you had been here, my brother would not have died" (John 11:21).

As we read those words, we feel what Martha must have felt—her deep sense of disappointment that Jesus had not shown up in time to use his power to heal her brother, Lazarus. She fully recognized that Jesus had the power to prevent death. But she seemed to think Jesus was limited by proximity, that he had to be there in person to do it. And he had not shown up in time.

But now Jesus was there. And it was as if Martha had a flicker of hope that defied the unpleasant realities of a decomposing body. She knew Jesus had raised some people from the dead during his ministry—but never someone who had been dead for four days. Even so, she ventured into that possibility, saying, "Even now I know that God will give you whatever you ask" (John 11:22). Perhaps Jesus might still use his influence with his Father to bring her brother's body back to life.

Then Jesus told her, "Your brother will rise again."
JOHN 11:23

Martha responded, "Yes, . . . he will rise when everyone else rises, at the last day" (John 11:24). She'd heard Jesus talk about a great day coming, and she believed that there would be a grand resurrection on that day far in the future. But she couldn't seem to find any comfort in it—at least not enough to balance out the pain she felt at that moment. Her response exposed her belief that resurrection was a completely future event, offering no comfort in the here and now of deep grief.

When Jesus told Martha her brother would rise again, I wonder if his words hit her like it hits us when someone tries to comfort us by telling us that the one we love is in heaven and that we will see him or her again one day. It's true and it helps a little, but honestly not enough. Heaven just feels so far away.

We have a hard time finding comfort in our future hope under the crush of present pain. Resurrection can seem so religious, so unreal, so far removed.

Martha couldn't find solace in the future tense. And those of us who have lost someone we love understand that, don't we? We have a hard time finding comfort in our future hope under the crush of present pain. Resurrection can seem so religious, so unreal, so far removed.

It was at this point that Jesus made a statement about himself that changed Martha's idea of resurrection from a purely future event into a present reality—a reality she could find rest and consolation in at that very moment, in her time of tremendous sorrow.

Jesus Talks about Who He Is

It was into Martha's dry doctrine, devoid of palpable comfort and hope, that Jesus said to her, "I am the resurrection and the life. Anyone who believes in me will live, even after dying.

Everyone who lives in me and believes in me will never ever die. Do you believe this, Martha?" (John 11:25-26).

When Jesus said he is the resurrection and the life, he was not only speaking about something he would do in the future. He was telling us who he is—the essence of who he is—not just who he will be, but who he is now and forever. He is not only life after death; he is life now. Jesus is life to our bodies and our souls. He is the source from which all life springs: "In him we live and move and exist" (Acts 17:28). Once we are made alive in Christ, our lives can never truly be extinguished.

When Jesus spoke these words to sorrowful Martha, he was saying that life doesn't end for the person who believes—that eternal life cannot be snuffed out and has actually already begun for anyone who has united himself or herself to him, the resurrection and the life. Jesus is not just the giver of victory over death in an obscure future. He provides victory over death in the actual present.

Those who believe in Jesus know that when physical death comes, as it does for each one of us, our bodies may be buried, but our souls go immediately into the presence of God. We also know that God will not leave our dead bodies in the earth forever. When he returns, he will reunite our souls with our bodies, changing them into glorified, perfected resurrection bodies like his own. While our physical bodies may be on a steady march toward death, in reality we are drawing ever closer into life as it was meant to be, in bodies fit for a new heaven and a new earth, where we will be together forever with the one we love most—Jesus himself.

Jesus Asks What You Believe

It is possible to have a theological understanding of resurrection life but to find no joy or comfort in it, to have no ability to rest in it, or to simply not believe it. And Jesus knows our belief in him as the resurrection and the life is pivotal—foundational— to how we face grief and sorrow.

That's why he followed up his statement about who he is with a penetrating question about what we believe. And I think it is the question Jesus would ask you today as he looks into your life and sees you seeking to make sense of who he is in your sorrow. "I am the resurrection and the life. . . . Do you believe this?"

Do you believe that one you love who died in Christ is now enjoying the presence of God, which is better by far than life in this world?

Do you believe that Jesus himself is the source for all life and that he can be trusted to infuse your present and your future with overflowing, unstoppable life?

Jesus repeatedly spoke about the importance of believing:

> *"Everyone who believes in him will not perish but*
> *have eternal life."*
>
> JOHN 3:16

"This is the only work God wants from you: Believe in the one he has sent."

JOHN 6:29

"The world's sin is that it refuses to believe in me."

JOHN 16:9

So perhaps we need to ask ourselves, *What does it mean to believe in Jesus?* Certainly believing is more than simply agreeing to a list of facts about who Jesus is and what he did, more than assenting to a set of theological tenets. To believe is to depend on those truths, rest in them, and put all our stock in them, holding nothing back. Belief begins when we agree with the truth about Jesus, and it blossoms into saving faith as we accept that truth for ourselves, entrusting our whole selves to Christ.

In the original language John wrote in, he didn't actually say we should "believe in" Jesus. Our Bibles say it that way because it would sound strange to our ears for the verse to read what Jesus was literally saying. Jesus' actual words were that we have to "believe into" him. To believe into Jesus is to enter into Jesus as a new way of living—to depend on him as our source of life—now and forever.

Earlier in his ministry Jesus said, "Unless you believe that I AM who I claim to be, you will die in your sins" (John 8:24). The crucible of belief separates those who are plunged into a dark forever separated from God and those who enter into an eternity overflowing with life and joy. Jesus was not content to settle for vague uncertainty like so many of us are today. That's why Jesus asked Martha this all-important question—"Do you believe?"—and it's why he asks you and me the same thing.

It is almost too direct a question, isn't it? It makes us a little uncomfortable. We are more comfortable with an inspirational kind of faith and an impersonal type of religion. It seems a bit pushy to be forced into answering the question. But Jesus is not afraid to push the issue of belief. He's loving us when he asks us this question, because he knows that what we believe makes an eternal difference.

Do you believe that Jesus is who he says he is—the resurrection and the life—and do you really believe that the person who believes in him is, even now, fully and forever alive?

"Well, I think so," we might say.

The truth is, if we really believe this, if we've really entered into this as a new way of life, it will make a difference in how we grieve when we lose someone we love. I'm not saying that belief has the power to take away all the pain. But it does change how we grieve—we don't grieve like people who have no hope (1 Thessalonians 4:13).

As David and I walked away from the grave after burying Hope, he said to me, "You know, I think we expected that our faith would make this hurt less, but it doesn't. Our faith gave us an incredible amount of strength and encouragement while we had her, and we are comforted by the knowledge that Hope is in heaven. Our faith keeps us from being swallowed by despair. But I don't think it makes our loss hurt any less."

In our experience, faith has not taken away the pain, but it has informed our thoughts and our emotions. It has infused our loss with purpose and hope.

If you believe what Jesus says about those who believe in him, you will grieve differently from those who do not believe. You will grieve as a person whose soul is anchored by confidence in God's promises. You'll grieve with a hope that is not based on wishful thinking, empty sentimentality, vague superstition, or pervasive denial, but on the solid foundation of who Jesus is (the resurrection and the life), what he has done (overcome death), and what he has promised (life that never ends).

If you believe that your loved one who has died in Christ is really more alive than ever, you will not get stuck in the mire of seeing death as a tragedy.

If you believe that your loved one who has died in Christ will experience the reality of a resurrected body in the new heaven and new earth, you will not get stuck in the mire of seeing death as a tragedy. You can begin to see it as an open door into unending joy.

If you believe in Jesus, you won't see death as the end—the end of a life, the end of your relationship with the one you love, the end of God's loving care for you. Instead, you'll see it as the beginning of life in the presence of God, where one day we'll have new hearts to love purely, new minds to think rightly, a new eternal purpose, and a new environment to live in that is not impacted by the damning effects of sin.

If you believe in Jesus, though you ache to have the one you love here with you, your love for that person and your confidence in the promises of God will actually help to turn this ache of sorrow into anticipation of joy. The reality of life beyond this world will become more real, and your longing for it will grow. Your thoughts of it will become less sentimental and more solid and sure.

When Jesus says, "Anyone who believes in me will live, even after dying," we realize that here is the real miracle we are looking for, even if our prayers are shortsighted. The reason this account of Lazarus's resurrection is in the Bible is not so we will long for the same bodily miracle he experienced, because Lazarus still died. Jesus raised Lazarus from the dead, not so Lazarus could get a second chance and not so Mary and Martha wouldn't have to grieve, but so that we would believe that Jesus is who he says he is, that he has power over death. Jesus raised Lazarus from the dead so that we can rest in his promise that if we believe in him we will live, even after our bodies die.

Eventually the day must have come when Mary and Martha went to the tomb again with the lifeless shell of what was once their beloved brother. That time there was no miraculous resurrection. But by then, their solid belief in Jesus as the resurrection and the life had blossomed into a restful trust. Lazarus's next funeral occurred this side of Easter, and because Jesus had risen from the dead, they believed that Lazarus would one day be resurrected too. That time, though they faced the grave with sorrow, it was a hope-filled sorrow devoid of despair. That time they faced his death with confidence that resurrection was not just a far-off religious exercise but a right-now personal experience.

It is perhaps the ultimate question of life. Certainly it is the most important question you and I have to answer as we work our way through grief and questions following the death of someone we love, or as we face our own unavoidable deaths.

How will we answer Jesus when we hear him speaking into our sorrow: "He who believes in me will live, even though he dies. . . . *Do you believe this?*"

As He Gives You Life That Never Ends

—— 🌿 ——

EVERY SPARK OF LIFE began with me. I am the life giver and life sustainer. I made humans out of dust and breathed the breath of life into them. And if you believe that, surely you can believe me when I tell you that my Spirit can give you life that will not end when your body goes back to the dust.

I am not waiting until some future date to start giving you this never-ending life. A new quality of life begins for you the moment you come to me. If you have me, you have life, even though death is all around you. Your life flows from mine, and my life cannot be snuffed out.

These are not empty words or empty promises. My words are spirit and life, so grab hold of them with all you've got. I'm inviting you to rest in who I am—life itself—and in what I've promised to you—rich, satisfying, unending life.

Trusting my promises takes faith. But I'm not talking about "blind faith" or a "leap of faith." You find the foundation for faith in the reality of my resurrection. I died and rose again so you would know that I have the power to lay my life down and also to take it up again. And I am promising you that same death-defying, life-giving power.

You can stake your life and your death on what I'm telling you. As you keep listening to my voice, you can face death without fear, confident that life is on the other side of death.

Adapted from Hebrews 1:3; Genesis 2:7; Acts 17:25; John 3:6; 1 John 5:12; John 14:6; 10:10; 6:63; 10:18

CHAPTER 10

HEAR JESUS SAYING,

I Am in Control of Your Life and Your Death

"Don't be afraid! . . . I hold the keys of death and the grave." REVELATION 1:17-18

Jesus soothes our fear of death.

I suppose none of us get through life without picking up some regrets along the way. And certainly I have accumulated my own collection. Although we did our best to live each day we were given with Hope and Gabe in ways that we would have no regrets, a few slipped in as unwelcomed guests. One regret I have is that I didn't spend enough time just being quiet with them, focused on them, taking in the feel of their skin against mine.

But I do remember one pivotal day when I spent some significant time sitting with Hope in her darkened nursery, rocking back and forth in the glider rocker our friends had given us. Feeling Hope's time with us slipping away far too quickly, I began to form the words in my mind to beg God to extend her life. My sense was that I had been very generous and gracious to God in accepting that Hope would not grow old with us, so it seemed a perfectly reasonable request on my part to ask God to extend her life, at least a little.

But before my prayer was fully formed, I was caught short. *Do I really want Hope to live any longer than God has intended for her?* I thought. Maybe a longer life would not be better for her or for me. Maybe it would mean more suffering for her. . . . It was a crossroads of a kind for me, at which I was forced to reckon with whether or not I would choose to trust God with the length of her life, whether or not I would trust that the number of days God gave her would be right for her, and for me.

I suppose I began thinking about that around the third day of Hope's life when, in a phone conversation in my hospital room, my friend Anne Graham Lotz told me, "The purpose for Hope's life will be completely accomplished in the number of days that God gives her." That was a profound truth to take in and one I grabbed hold of and hung on to. It added significance and meaning to Hope's limited little life.

Then I read *The Last Thing We Talk About* by Joseph Bayly, who lost three children—one at eighteen days, after surgery; another at five years, from leukemia; the third at eighteen years, after a sledding accident. Bayly wrote, "Shortly after our five-year-old died of leukemia, someone asked me how I'd feel if a cure for leukemia were then discovered. My short answer was that I'd be thankful, but it would be irrelevant to the death of my son. God determined to take him to His home at the age of five; the means was incidental."

The profound truth of his statement struck a chord deep within me. It shaped my thinking and calmed my desperation. It soothed my fear about the reality of death closing in on us. My growing confidence that God was in control of Hope's life and death gave me peace.

I wonder if it was that same sense of confidence in God's control that gave the apostle John peace as his final days were slipping away while he was imprisoned on the remote island of Patmos. We read about it in Revelation 1.

> *I, John, am your brother and your partner in suffering and in God's Kingdom and in the patient endurance to which Jesus calls us. I was exiled to the island of Patmos for preaching the word of God and for my testimony about Jesus.*
>
> REVELATION 1:9

As a prisoner on Patmos, John probably spent his days, at ninety years of age, doing manual labor. History tells us that in the marble mines on the Isle of Patmos, men worked chained to their "slave barrows." John probably didn't have a real bed to sleep in or adequate food to eat or enough clean water to drink. He likely had no salve for the sores that developed as he worked day in and day out in the rocky terrain. And if we think about people we know who are ninety years old, we have to wonder if his joints ached from arthritis and if he suffered other ailments of old age. Surely he felt the pain of sorrow and loneliness, as most of his fellow apostles had faced martyrs' deaths long before.

The voice of Jesus speaking into John's sorrow was loud and unavoidable, powerful and penetrating.

When we find John in Revelation, it is the Lord's Day, and rather than obsessing about his situation, John is spending time listening to hear Jesus speak to him.

It was the Lord's Day, and I was worshiping in the Spirit.
REVELATION 1:10

John was likely listening for that still, small voice of God's Spirit to whisper comfort or assurance of his presence in that painful place. But that day, a still, small voice is not what John heard. He writes, "I heard behind me a loud voice like a trumpet" (Revelation 1:10). In that moment, the voice of Jesus speaking into John's sorrow was loud and unavoidable, powerful and penetrating.

John writes that he "turned to see who was speaking to me" (Revelation 1:12). When we think about John seeing Jesus, we realize he had already seen Jesus. He had already heard the voice of Jesus. He had spent three years with Jesus. He had rested his head against Jesus. He had stood at the foot of the cross as Jesus hung there and committed himself to take care of Jesus' mother. He had seen Jesus cooking breakfast on the seashore. And he had seen Jesus ascend into heaven. But what he saw and heard that day on Patmos was dramatically different.

"I saw," he says, "someone like the Son of Man" (Revelation 1:12-13). In other words, John saw someone who looked completely human yet radiant with the splendor of heaven. He described the magnificent, glorified Jesus in the most tangible terms he could come up with:

> *His head and his hair were white like wool, as white as snow. And his eyes were like flames of fire. His feet were like polished bronze refined in a furnace, and his voice thundered like mighty ocean waves. He held seven stars in his right hand, and a sharp two-edged sword came from his mouth. And his face was like the sun in all its brilliance.*
>
> REVELATION 1:14-16

The sight of Jesus in his glorified humanity was startling. It was stunning. It was silencing. In this conversation with Jesus, John was speechless. He didn't *say* anything. But what he *did* was telling.

Verse 17 describes John's reaction: "When I saw him, I fell at his feet as if I were dead." John fell down before Jesus in worship and wonder and submission and stillness—which is the only appropriate response to seeing Jesus as he truly is and hearing his voice as it truly sounds.

"He laid his right hand on me," John recounts. When Jesus reached out to touch him, Jesus said, "Don't be afraid! I am the First and the Last. I am the living one. I died, but look—I am alive forever and ever! And I hold the keys of death and the grave" (Revelation 1:17-18). When Jesus told John and you and me that he is "the First and the Last," he was saying, "Everything started with me, and everything will end with me. You find your starting point and your ending place completely in me."

Do you really believe God is in control of both the beginning and the ending of your life, and every day in between? Evidently David the psalmist did. He put it this way:

> *You watched me as I was being formed in utter*
> *seclusion,*
> > *as I was woven together in the dark of the womb.*
> > *You saw me before I was born.*
> > *Every day of my life was recorded in your book.*
> > *Every moment was laid out*
> > *before a single day had passed.*
>
> PSALM 139:15-16

These verses tell us that God has ordained or planned everything that happens in our world from before Creation. And though it is impossible for us to fully fathom how God knows everything in advance without taking away from our freedom or responsibility, we see his complete providential control of human history throughout the pages of Scripture.

But I have to admit that this is easier to accept in the big picture than it is in daily details. On the days when life seems good, it is easy to say to God, "Every day of my life was recorded in your book." But on the day tragedy strikes, on the day our lives are changed forever by loss, on the day we discover the infidelity or

The person who holds the keys controls access. The person with the keys opens and closes.

get the final test results or say good-bye for the last time, we wonder, *Was this day of my life written in your book, by your hand? Is this the story you intended to write for my life, or has there been a terrible mistake?*

This is where we need to hear Jesus speaking to us, assuring us of his providential control, reminding us not to be afraid. This is where we need to hear Jesus tell us what he told John— that he "hold[s] the keys of death and the grave."

What does it mean that Jesus holds the keys to death and the grave? The person who holds the keys controls access. The person with the keys opens and closes.

Imagine what this meant to John as he wasted away on Patmos, perhaps wondering if he would die there. Imagine what it meant to the believers in those early churches who would read John's record of this encounter with Jesus. They had seen their loved ones taken from them and thrown to the lions, as they no doubt wondered if they would be next in line. Imagine the comfort and confidence it must have given them to hear Jesus say that he is in charge of life and death. These penetrating words coming out of the mouth of the glorified, resurrected Jesus assured them that they didn't have to be afraid that someone or something might take their lives, or the lives of those they loved, prematurely.

When you face the death of someone you love, you don't have to surrender that person to an unknown, uncaring nothingness.

And neither do we.

Because Jesus is in charge of life and death. Jesus assures us that he has the keys in his hands to the place of the dead. No one goes there unless and until he opens that door. He holds the keys because he died and went there himself and emerged with the keys in his hand.

Jesus Speaks into Our Fear of Death

Can you hear the powerful, penetrating voice of Jesus speaking this promise to your own heart today? "Don't be afraid," he says to you, "I hold the keys of death."

This means that no matter what the doctor says about how much time you have left, you will live exactly the number of days God has ordained for you. This means that when that person you loved died in an awful accident, it didn't catch God by surprise. It means that even though it seems like the one you loved died much too soon, it was really right on time.

This means you can surrender all the if-onlys that taunt you in your thoughts—*If only he had gone to the doctor earlier, If only I had warned her, If only he had stayed home that day, If only I had been a better witness, If only I had seen the signs.*

Jesus himself controls life and death.

This means that when you face the death of someone you love, you don't have to surrender that person to an unknown, uncaring nothingness. You can rest, knowing that the person you love who knows Jesus is safely in his care and under his loving control. Jesus holds the keys.

Even if you aren't sure about your loved one's relationship to Jesus, you can be confident in the character of the one who holds the keys, trusting that he will do what is right, remembering that the heart of the one who holds the keys is full of mercy.

And as you face your own death, which may seem far away or very close, Jesus reaches out to touch you and comfort you in your fear, reminding you that he holds the keys. Death cannot catch him off guard or sneak up on him. He is in control.

When we're confident that Jesus is in control of our lives and our deaths, we don't have to be afraid. We can surrender our need to always be in control, confident that Jesus not only holds the keys, he holds us as well.

As He Shows You How to Face Death without Fear

————————— 🌿 —————————

IT IS NATURAL TO BE afraid of death. But if you are in me, you are no longer living life or facing death in the natural way. You can face death with supernatural confidence—confidence that everything I've promised is really true and that everything you've placed your hopes in is really real. This confidence comes from being convinced that nothing can separate you from my Father's love—not even death.

Find your rest in my promises and your peace in following my example. Remember my words as I faced death, when I cried out from the cross, "Father, I entrust my spirit into your hands!" and entrust your spirit into his hands too. Shout from the depths of your soul with the psalmist, "My future is in your hands!"

Your life is in your Father's hands, and your death is in his hands. The deaths of those you love are in his hands. And because of that you can rest, knowing there is no safer place to be when you are mine than in my hands.

Adapted from Hebrews 2:14-15; 6:18; 11:1; Titus 3:6-7; Romans 8:38; Luke 23:46; Psalm 31:15; 1 Peter 2:23

Conclusion

HEAR JESUS SAYING,
I Will Give You Rest

"Come to me, all of you who are weary and carry heavy burdens, and I will give you rest." MATTHEW 11:28

Jesus opens his arms to us.

My friend Angela and I were coming up the walkway to my house when David came out to greet us.

"You have some bad news," I said to him instinctively.

He told us that he had just gotten a phone call that some friends' young daughter had been struck by a car in their driveway, and she was being airlifted to the hospital. We instantly developed a sick feeling in our stomachs—for the girl, for her parents, and for whoever was driving the car—and we began to pray for all of them.

Then the phone rang again, telling us that the little girl had died. We hopped in the car and headed to the hospital, where we found a room full of friends who were shocked and sad and unsure of what to say or do. When the family came into the room after saying good-bye to the body of their precious daughter and sister, they went from one set of arms to another, leaning into people who love them, shedding tears and seeking solace.

This was a moment when no words needed to be spoken. There was no rush to theologize or explain. It was a time for arms to be open, for tears to be shed, and for the very presence of those in the room to speak of their promise to be there in the days ahead to help shoulder the load of grief.

It was a picture of the promise I see in Jesus' words in Matthew 11:

> *Jesus said, "Come to me, all of you who are weary*
> *and carry heavy burdens, and I will give you rest.*
> *Take my yoke upon you. Let me teach you, because*
> *I am humble and gentle at heart, and you will find*
> *rest for your souls. For my yoke is easy to bear, and the*
> *burden I give you is light."*
> MATTHEW 11:28-30

Can you hear him speaking to you personally through these words? Can you see Jesus opening his arms to you, waiting to envelop you, providing a safe place for you to let it all out?

The burden of sorrow you've been carrying may seem too heavy to keep shouldering on your own. Jesus opens his arms to you and invites you into himself, where you can rest.

When he says, "Take my yoke upon you," he's not putting you to work. He's inviting you to share the yoke that is also around his neck. He is offering to shoulder the load as you connect yourself to him. He will do the heavy lifting of the burden that is pressing in on you, crushing you.

Hear his promise to be there in the days ahead to help shoulder the load of sorrow in your heart.

And when he says, "Let me teach you," hear his heart, which is humble and gentle. He doesn't bark orders or drill us for the perfect answer. He teaches us through his words and through his example, inviting us into his way of living, his way of understanding, his way of loving. Only in him will we find the rest we long for.

In the midst of your heartache, Jesus will hold you in his arms, he will teach you, and he will speak into your sorrow. Hear his promise to be there in the days ahead to help shoulder the load of sorrow in your heart.

"The very words I have spoken to you are spirit and life," Jesus said (John 6:63).

May the Spirit impress the truth of what Jesus has said deep into your heart, changing how you feel. May you find life in his words as they take root in your mind, changing how you think. In his words, and in his arms, may you find rest for your sorrowful soul.

Discussion Guide

CHAPTER 1: **Hear Jesus Saying, *I, Too, Have Known Overwhelming Sorrow*** (Matthew 26:38)

Jesus understands the crushing weight and agonizing loneliness of grief.

- What does it mean to hear Jesus speak, and how can you really do that? How do you know it is his voice you are hearing?

- Does it help you to know that Jesus has experienced overwhelming sorrow and agonizing loneliness? In what ways?

- What truths do you find in Hebrews 2:14-18 that add to your understanding of Jesus sharing your sorrow?

- What specific aspects of your experience of sorrow do you think Jesus is able or unable to identify with?

- How can seeing and hearing from Jesus as the Man of Sorrows change how you pray and how you worship?

CHAPTER 2: **Hear Jesus Saying,** *I, Too, Have Heard God Tell Me No* (MATTHEW 26:39)

Jesus shows us what to do when God doesn't give us what we want.

- How do you relate to Nancy's struggle to reconcile God's sovereignty and power with his compassion toward us in our sorrow?

- It can be difficult to embrace the humanness of Jesus that is evident in his desire for something different from what God wanted. How does the reality of his struggle give you hope?

- What did Jesus know about his suffering and about God that enabled him to surrender?

- In what way(s) do you sense God has said no to you? And how have you responded to that so far?

- How is it possible to move from the place of insisting that God fulfill our requests to submitting to God so we can say, "I want your will to be done, not mine"?

- First Peter 2:23 says that Jesus "entrusted himself to him who judges justly" (NIV) or that he "left his case in the hands of God" (NLT). What will it take for you to be able to do that, and what do you think it would look like as you live that out?

CHAPTER 3: **Hear Jesus Saying,** *I Am Willing to Heal Your Deadliest Disease* (MARK 1:41)

Jesus knows what we need most of all.

- How can you relate to this statement: "Those of us who do not get the physical healing we prayed for can be left assuming that either our faith is deficient or God is unable or unwilling to heal us or the one we love. And in some ways, a surface-level tour through the Gospels can add to that assumption"?

- How does John 20:30-31 inform your understanding of the miracles of Jesus?

- How can you welcome God's healing work in your life right now while recognizing that we are living in that in-between time when we get a taste of his healing power but do not know it in its fullness?

- Why do you think we tend to see God's willingness to heal us of our deadly disease of sin as somehow less than the physical healing we want from him?

- What does it really mean to see our sin as our most significant sickness, and how does that change the way we relate to God?

CHAPTER 4: **Hear Jesus Saying, *I Will Save You from Yourself*** (MATTHEW 16:23)

Jesus saves us from a wasted life of trying to get our own way.

- How do you respond to this statement: "The assumption that God should give faithful believers a comfortable life, and certainly no more than one dose of sorrow, seems to be an American-made version of the Christian life that doesn't hold up to examination"?

- Think through and discuss specific faithful followers of God in the Bible. What were their lives like? Did they make following God look good to the world?

- Read the following passages: 1 Corinthians 3:18-23 and 2 Corinthians 6:4-10. How do they illustrate the paradox of living the Christian life, and how do they reveal the ways in which our human perspective is different from God's perspective?

- Is it realistic to think you could begin to see things from God's perspective rather than merely from a human point of view? If so, how does that happen?

- What do you think it means to "turn from your selfish ways, take up your cross, and follow" Jesus here and now (Matthew 16:24)?

CHAPTER 5: **Hear Jesus Saying,** *I Will Keep You Safe*
(MATTHEW 10:28)

Jesus protects us from eternal harm.

- What promises of God have you sought to claim in your sorrow, and how do you see or foresee God fulfilling those promises?

- What should you assume if it appears that God has failed to live up to a promise he has made?

- How are you challenged when you hear Jesus speaking to his disciples, telling us that we should not be concerned about anyone or anything that can kill our bodies, since they cannot touch our souls (Matthew 10:28)?

- Jesus prays we will be protected from the evil one. What does the evil one want to do to us (Mark 4:15; Luke 22:31-32; John 8:44; 1 Peter 5:8)?

- Does the promise that Jesus has protected you from the wrath of God that you deserve move you or cause you to feel a deep sense of gratitude? If not, why might that be?

- What can you do with your disappointment that God does not promise to protect you and those you love from all physical harm here and now? And how can you grow in your appreciation for his promise to protect your soul for eternity?

CHAPTER 6: **Hear Jesus Saying,** *I Have a Purpose in Your Pain* (JOHN 9:3)

Jesus gives us insight when we wonder why.

- How do you relate to this statement: "There is something deep inside us that tells us that we get what we deserve, or maybe that we deserve what we get"? Have you ever sensed that your suffering was God's way of making you pay for your sin?

- What is the difference between seeing your suffering as discipline from God and as punishment from God?

- Nancy says, "The same tool of suffering that Satan seeks to use to *destroy* our faith is, in the hands of God, a tool God plans to use to *develop* our faith. The same circumstance that Satan sends to tempt us to reject God is what God uses to train us. What Satan inflicts to wound us, God intends to prune us." How can embracing this truth change how you respond to your suffering?

- How does considering God's role in the suffering of Joseph, Job, Israel, and Jesus challenge and inform your understanding of God's role in your own suffering?

- How does thinking about the causes and purposes of suffering as presented in this chapter help you as you seek to understand the causes and purposes of your own suffering?

CHAPTER 7: **Hear Jesus Saying,** *I Will Give You a Heart for Forgiveness* (MARK 11:25)

Jesus empowers us to forgive people who don't deserve it.

- What are some of the ways we tend to justify our resentments? And what fears make us slow to grant forgiveness?

- What is the difference between someone sinning against you and someone merely hurting or offending you? Is there any difference between how you forgive in each situation?

- Many people say that forgiveness is not required or is not complete unless the person who has hurt you asks for forgiveness. How does that requirement hold us hostage to our burning resentment? What is the difference between forgiveness and reconciliation?

- Think about people you know who have allowed unforgiveness to take root in their lives. How has that shaped who they are and how they relate to others?

- What do you think it means that "forgiveness is choosing to absorb the pain and pay the debt yourself that you are rightfully owed, asking God to do a work of grace and quench the fiery anger in your heart"?

- What is one step toward forgiveness, however small, that you could take now to begin to relinquish your resentment?

CHAPTER 8: Hear Jesus Saying, *I Am Enough for You*

(2 CORINTHIANS 12:9)

Jesus provides what we need when we need it.

- In what ways have you felt emptiness in your sorrow?

- When you read about Paul's experience with the thorn, does it encourage you or disappoint you? Why?

- How does seeing that the thorn was a messenger of Satan sent to torment Paul but also a tool of God sent to protect Paul from pride cause you to see your own suffering as perhaps something Satan has sent to harm you but that God can use to help you?

- In what ways do you need the grace of Jesus to be sufficient for you? How will you know that it is enough?

- What is the difference between praying that a thorn will be removed and praying that it will be redeemed?

CHAPTER 9: **Hear Jesus Saying,** *I Am Giving Life to Those Who Believe in Me* (JOHN 11:25-26)

Jesus asks us to believe that death is not the end of life.

- How do you relate to Martha's inability to find comfort in the resurrection as a completely future event or as merely religious but not real?

- How does Jesus' promise that "anyone who believes in me will live, even after dying" (John 11:25) relate to other things Jesus said that we have looked at in previous chapters, such as his willingness to heal us of our most deadly disease—sin—or his being more concerned about our eternal souls than our physical bodies?

- How does a person know if his or her belief has moved beyond simply agreeing to a list of facts about Jesus and into genuine saving faith?

- How do you think Mary and Martha's experience of grieving the death of their brother would have been different the second time he died?

- Has believing that Jesus is the resurrection and life made a difference in how you have grieved? If so, how? If not, why not?

CHAPTER 10: **Hear Jesus Saying,** *I Am in Control of Your Life and Your Death* (REVELATION 1:17-18)

Jesus soothes our fear of death.

- How can the truth that God has ordained the number of our days soothe our fears about life and death?

- Notice that one of the first things Jesus said to John in Revelation was, "Don't be afraid." Why do you think he said that, and how can it help you to hear Jesus saying those words to you?

- What are the significant implications of embracing the belief of the psalmist that "every day of my life was recorded in your book. Every moment was laid out before a single day had passed" (Psalm 139:16)?

- How does your confidence that Jesus holds the keys to life and death help you deal with regrets? How does it soothe your fears?

Conclusion: **Hear Jesus Saying,** *I Will Give You Rest*
(MATTHEW 11:28)

Jesus opens his arms to us.

- How does it help you not only to hear Jesus inviting you to himself but also to see him with his arms open to you?

- How is grief and sorrow a heavy load, and what would it mean to know that Jesus is offering to shoulder the load with you?

- What do you need rest from in your sorrow, and how can you receive that rest by coming to Jesus?

ACKNOWLEDGMENTS

I am grateful to Umbrella Ministries, which invited me to speak at their annual retreat for women who have lost children, where I first gave the message that laid the foundation for this book. How well I remember reading through the list of women who would be at the retreat along with the names of their children and their causes of death. The magnitude of their sorrow took my breath away. It still does. It made me desperate to offer something beyond squishy sentimentality—a genuine hope and truth to hold on to, which I found in listening for the voice of Jesus.

I'm grateful to Michelle Alm, who continues to inspire and challenge me. Michelle pointed me in the direction of writing this book and encouraged me that there was something here worth saying. Thank you to Jan Long Harris for catching the vision, to Stephanie Voiland for helping the vision take shape, and to Nancy Clausen, Yolanda Sidney, and Sharon Leavitt for helping it take flight. Thank you to the faithful sales team at Tyndale for continuing to believe in my ministry.

I am indebted to Dr. Wilson Benton for giving me some needed correction and to Randy Alcorn for his helpful input.

This book also benefited from feedback from my friends Nancy Langham, Karen Anderson, and Stephanie Seefeldt and from my most valued and gentle critic, David Guthrie. My name may be on the cover, but everything here is what he and I have been working out together as we've sought to make sense of our loss in light of Scripture.

One of the first things I remember saying to David when we met was, "You have a really great voice," and I still love to hear it. His is the voice I want to hear when I wake up in the morning and when my eyes close in sleep at night, second only to the voice of Jesus.

And I never want to stop hearing the voice of Jesus speaking into my sorrow—at least not until that day when sorrow is no more, when he will wipe away my tears for good.

Books by Nancy Guthrie

Holding On to Hope
978-1-4143-1296-5

Hearing Jesus Speak
into Your Sorrow
978-1-4143-2548-4

Hoping for Something Better
978-1-4143-1307-8

When Your Family's
Lost a Loved One
978-1-58997-480-7

The One Year Book of Hope
978-1-4143-0133-4 (softcover)
978-1-4143-3671-8 (leatherlike)

One Year of Dinner Table
Devotions and Discussion
Starters
978-1-4143-1895-0

Let Every Heart Prepare
Him Room
978-1-4143-3909-2

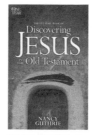

The One Year Book of
Discovering Jesus in the
Old Testament
978-1-4143-3590-2

Abundant Life in Jesus
978-1-4964-0948-5

For more information on these titles, visit www.tyndale.com or www.nancyguthrie.com.
For information about David and Nancy Guthrie's Respite Retreats for couples who have
faced the loss of a child, go to www.nancyguthrie.com/respite-retreat.

CP0066